DIRECTORY

OF THE

BOROUGH OF CHESTER, Penn.

FOR THE YEARS 1859-60;

CONTAINING A

Concise History of the Borough

FROM ITS FIRST SETTLEMENT TO THE PRESENT TIME; THE NAMES OF ALL THE INHABITANTS, ALPHABETICALLY ARRANGED, THEIR OCCUPATIONS, PLACES OF BUSINESS, AND DWELLING HOUSES; A LIST OF THE STREETS OF THE BOROUGH; STATISTICS OF PUBLIC AND PRIVATE SCHOOLS; THE LOCATION AND TIME OF HOLDING SERVICE IN THE CHURCHES; THE TIME OF ARRIVAL AND DEPARTURE OF THE DIFFERENT LINES OF TRAVEL; THE TIME AND PLACE OF MEETING OF THE VARIOUS SOCIETIES AND ASSOCIATIONS.

ALSO, THE CARDS OF THE PRINCIPAL MERCHANTS, ARTIZANS AND PROFESSIONAL MEN OF THE BOROUGH.

WILLIAM WHITEHEAD, Publisher.

WEST CHESTER:
E. F. James, Steam Power Book and Job Printer.
1859.

PREFACE.

In presenting to the people of Chester its History and Directory, the author is fully aware of the failure to arrive at perfect accuracy of detail. As it regards the History, he has only *attempted* its narration. A perfect History of the Borough, embracing varied, and wide ranges of interest, would require time, care, long and thorough research; such as none but an enthusiastic antiquarian would undertake. He can only hope that in pioneering the way, he may induce some one of much better investigating and literary ability to carry out to its proper completion the labor that is only begun.

W. W.

HISTORICAL SKETCH.

THE BOROUGH OF CHESTER,

The most ancient town and county seat in Pennsylvania, is situated upon the right bank of the Delaware river, in the south-eastern part of the State, 15 miles south-west of the city of Philadelphia. Its latitude north is 39° 50′ 45″, longitude from Washington 1° 39′ 27″ east, and from Greenwich 75° 22′ 05″ west. It was constituted a corporate town as early as 1690. The corporate limits are bounded on the north and west by Chester township, east by Ridley creek, and south by the Delaware river. Its territorial dimensions are two miles from east to west, and one and a quarter from north to south, containing about 1610 acres.

It stands upon a strip of alluvion running from one half to one mile from the river, formed by its receding waters. The upper stratum of clay lies upon a formation of aggregated rock of primitive character, of which Gneiss is the prevailing variety. This granitic structure crops out upon the banks of the creeks, furnishing solid and compact material for building and other purposes. About half a mile inland, and running westward from Ridley creek, embracing 40 or 50 acres, immediately beneath the clay lies a stratum of decomposed reeds, intermixed with mud, resembling turf in quality, being fusible like that material. The superstratum of clay is of fine quality and its depth in some places reaches 14 feet; affording a most abundant supply of material for the manufacture of brick, of which the buildings of modern date are almost solely constructed.

The great highway of travel and communication, previous to the era of railroads, was the broad and sweeping Delaware, whose tides so constantly bear the whitened sails of commerce and throw into the luxurious lap of the more fortunate metropolis of the state, the fabrics and wealth of distant climes. Opposite the town the river is over one mile in width, with a channel thirty-two feet in depth, bordered by a country enriched by the labor of industrious and skillful husbandry. Chester and Ridley creeks, which empty into the Delaware here, within three-fourths of a mile of each other, and into which its tides run for three miles, are available to a profitable extent for the transportation of tonnage; and the former, winding almost through the heart of the town, enables the river craft to enter and land their freights near the center of trade.

In the time of the early settlements, the channel of the Delaware ran quite near the northern shore, and vessels could approach the bank and be secured to the trees which grew upon it. As society and its wants increased, this aspect of the shore changed. The main cause of the change was the construction of two piers. The time at which the first were constructed is not known; but about the year 1815, those at Market and Edgmont streets, running out 500 feet beyond high water mark, were constructed. The channel being thus thrown farther from the shore, the space between the piers, as also the spaces upon either side, became the depositories of mud and detritus held in solution, from which has sprung a rank growth of reeds, presenting a view quite uninteresting. Land thus in the process of formation will eventually be reclaimed for useful purposes, and the now unsightly mud yet become localities for the thronged avenues of trade.

DELAWARE RIVER—DISCOVERY.

The Indians called the Delaware Lenape Wihittuck, or "the rapid stream of the Lenape;" the Dutch called it the South River, in contradistinction to the Hudson, or North River. Its present name was given in honor of Lord Delaware, who died at its capes in 1618. In an official report by a Dutch Chamber in 1644, it was claimed that the "South River was visited in 1598, and two forts erected upon it." Sir Walter Raleigh and Lord Delaware are likewise claimed as discoverers; but it is not probable that the former ever was in the country, and as the latter did not visit the bay until 1610, one year after the visit of Hudson, his claim could not be recognized. The discovery of its bay, or embouchure, we believe is fairly attributed to Hendrick Hudson, who entered it in the ship Crescent, on the 28th of August, 1609. It does not appear that he pursued his way up the bay any great distance, thus leaving to other adventurers the exploration of its waters amid the higher regions fringed by primeval forest.

The river was thus spoken of in 1656—"This river Delaware is considered the finest of all North America, being wide, deep, and navigable; abounding in fish, especially an abundance of *sturgeons*, of whose roes a great quantity of *cavejar* might be made.

Though settlements were made by the Dutch at Manhattan, now New York city, as early as 1610, no settlements upon the Delaware were known to exist prior to 1623; when Cornelius May, with a colony from Holland, entered the river, and sailed as far up as Gloucester, on the Jersey shore. May built a fort which he called Fort Nassau, for protection against the Indians. The colony failed of its object, and its members moved to the vicinity of the North River.

The next settlement attempted by the Dutch was under the lead of De Vries, who landed at Lewis' creek, near Cape Henlopen, in 1631. This settlement was likewise a failure, its members having been cut off by the vengeance of the Indians.

SWEDES.

The first colony of Swedes was planted in the spring of 1638, by Minuit, under the patronage of Queen Christina. The colonists landed at Christina, (now Wilmington,) and took the usual precaution of building means of defence.

The next in historical order, was a settlement by a few English families at Salem, in 1640, or 1641. But they were soon expelled by the united influence and remonstrances of the Dutch and Swedes. In the same year an English exploring party went as high up as the river Schuylkill, and entering that river, took possession and began the cultivation of the soil. As in the former case the Dutch, jealous of their jurisdiction, took successful measures for the expulsion of these settlers.

The second effort of the Swedes to plant a colony upon the shores of the Delaware, was in 1643, under John Printz, a Lieutenant Colonel in the service of Queen Christina. He fixed upon the pleasant spot known as Tinicum, the present site of the Lazaretto, where its bold shore, broad expanse of river, navigable creek and inviting country, courted the stay of the emigrant. The settlement was named New Gottenburg. Printz was a man of energy and determination, and within a year after his arrival had erected three forts, one at Christina, one at Tinicum and one at Elsinburgh, the latter being at the mouth of Salem creek.

At Upland many of the Swedes derived their titles to land from the Duke of York; as deeds from him are extant, of the date of 1668. The precise time of settlement, or under whose leadership it was effected, no dates, we believe, can verify; but it could not have been much later than those of their countrymen east and west of them; and the most truthful supposition is, that the spot was settled by offshoots from New Jersey, Christina and Tinicum: in other words, the Swedes spread themselves 'all along shore,' founding settlements where localities seemed inviting and eligible. This seems to be confirmed by Day, who, in speaking of the settlement of Printz, says,—"small hamlets were settled at various places along the shore and further inland."

Controversies between the Dutch and Swedes commenced early for right of possession and possession itself. They spread over many years, requiring too much detail for an extended examination. By right of discovery, settlement and treaties with the natives, the former claimed from Manhattan southward upon both sides of the Delaware river as far as its capes; the latter claimed, likewise, by discovery and settlement, and as they founded colonies upon the river, collisions, with varying success to each party, was the consequence. Notwithstanding this, time and intercourse softened down their mutual asperity, and in all these settlements Dutch and Swedes lived together, the intermixture gradually producing relations of amity and social regard. When Penn arrived at New Castle and Upland, they were found in this condition, and jointly welcomed the new ruler.

As the Dutch claimed almost as "large a charter as the wind," when the prevailing power of England dispossessed them of all their American possessions, the latter government also took ample scope and verge, with no boundary southward. The Lion laid his paw with emphatic force upon every rood claimed by former belligerents, and prepared to rule all their previous possessions. The fall of Manhattan was the signal of acquiescence every where, on the part of those who sought the triumph of Sweden or Holland.

The Indian name of the settlement at Chester was

MECOPONACA; the Swedes named it UPLAND, after a province of Sweden, upon the Gulf of Bothnia. Its change to Chester is said to have been under the following circumstances:—Shortly after the arrival of Penn, turning to his friend Pearson, who had been a companion of his voyage, he said, "Providence has brought us here safely; thou hast been the companion of my toils; what wilt thou that I should call this place?" Pearson replied "CHESTER, in remembrance of the city from whence I came." Penn replied, "it shall be called Chester, and when I divide the land into counties I will call one of them by the same name also."

Says Ferris, "it was a considerable town in 1682;" and the Rev. Mr. Hall, a very candid writer, in speaking of its condition in 1696, says, "Chester is mentioned as one of the four great market towns, and as 'mightily enlarged in this latter improvement.' But it is hardly presumable that at either of these dates, it could have numbered many inhabitants, as in 1672 Ferris states that "the country between Amboy and New Castle was a wilderness, and the site of Philadelphia inhabited by Indians. Travellers, in order to avoid rivers and creeks, passed inland several miles from the Delaware." It is stated, too, in reference to that period, "that the Swedish settlement at Upland is not mentioned." Campanius says, "there was a fort built there some time after its settlement," and Ferris adds, "But as no mention is made, by any other chronicler, of a fortification or regular military station at Upland, it is probable that *fort*, in this case, must be understood to mean a ***strong house***, or place of security in case of a sudden attack by the Indians. Such houses are often mentioned by the writers of that time." "The house of defence at Upland" is spoken of in 1677, in which year it was ordered to be fitted for the use of the Court.

National and religious ties kept the Swedes a homogeneous people in the new settlements, long preserving their habits and customs. Says Mr. Rudman in 1697, "we live scattered among the English and Quakers, yet our language is preserved as pure as any where in Sweden: there are about 1200 persons that speak it." They were treated by the Indians with great consideration, in relation to which the Rev. Eric Biork observes—"the Indians and we are as one people; we live in much greater friendship with them than with the English; they call the Swedes in their language, their own people." Penn regarded them as among the original settlers of the country; pioneers in the path of adventure and suffering, and received them upon his landing "with great kindness." Upon that occasion Captain Lasse Cock, was deputed by them, as a distinct people, to address the Proprietor on their behalf. He did so, assuring Penn that "they would love, serve and obey him with all they possessed." To show his confidence in them, two of their countrymen, Anders Bengtson and Sven Svenson, were appointed among the members of the first Assembly, and Penn's description of them is, "they are plain, strong, industrious people. They kindly received me, as well as the English, who were but few before the people concerned with me came among them. I must needs commend their respect to authority and kind behavior to the English."

Whilst the Dutch held a short sway over the settlements upon the Delaware in 1763, they were divded into three counties or judicial districts. The most northern was Upland, its seat having the same name. This division was continued under the English Govnor, Andross.

INDIAN TRIBES.

The Indian Tribes upon the Delaware river were the *Lenni Lenape*, signifying *original people.* The nation was divided into three principal tribes, under the respective titles of the Unamis or Turtle, Unalachtgos or Turkeys, and Monseys or Wolf; which were subdivided into numerous subordinate tribes. The Algonquin was their common language, variously modified by dialects, probably springing from the variations of locality, intercourse with neighboring tribes, and the adoption of phrases from the fragments of stranger tribes that sought their protection or alliance. Among the traditions of the Lenape was one of a character somewhat obscure, yet extant during the early settlements of the Swedes, to the effect that their nation had come from the setting sun, the west, and conquered a people, whose mounds, scattered over the great western valley, give evidence of a nation of higher civilization than could be accorded to the Indian race.

The Unamis and Unalachtgos occupied the country along the coast, between the sea and the Blue Mountains; and their settlements extended from the Hudson to the Potomac. Among the settlers they were known as the Delaware Indians, and doubtless were the same whose council fires lighted the waves of the lordly river, the banks of which the early pioneers of civilization sought as a homestead. They kindly welcomed the peaceful followers of Fox, and the testimony of Penn is, that "In liberality they excel; nothing is too good for their friend; give them a fine gun, coat, or other thing, it may pass twenty hands before it sticks; light of heart, strong affections, but soon spent. The most merry creatures that live, feast and dance perpetually; they never have much, nor want much; wealth circulateth like blood; all parts partake; and though none shall want what another hath, yet exact observers of property."

ARRIVAL OF PENN.

To seek an asylum for the members of his faith was prominent among the motives of Penn, in first visiting the New World. His charter for the Province of Pennsylvania, obtained from Charles II, is dated March 4th, 1681. He embarked for his province in 1682, in the ship Welcome, commanded by Capt. Greenaway, and arrived at New Castle on the 27th of October, of that year, where he was welcomed with much affection by those who represented the various nations of which the colony was composed. Says Duponceau, "English, Welsh, Dutch, Germans and Indians, all crowded to hail the great man whom they had been expecting for one long year, and whose fame had already preceded him to these distant regions." The *Lenni Lenape*, likewise, had their representative in the person of the great *Tamanend*, "who," says the same gifted author, "is said never to have had his equal for virtue and goodness."

Penn landed at Upland in the early part of November, but a few days after that at New Castle. Here, with his friends, he was received with similar demonstrations of regard, and hospitably entertained by Robert Wade, a leading and wealthy Friend, who resided very near the spot where the landing was effected, and owned land for some distance back into the country. Wade's was known as the Essex House, and stood upon the site of the commodius brick house now at the northwest corner of Penn and Front streets, owned and occupied by Capt. Rich. Ross, and which was built by Jesse M. Eyre, in 1850. The southeast gable of Wade's house fronted the river Delaware, its southwest front was towards Essex street, and its front porch looked out upon Chester creek. It was about two hundred yards from where Chester creek now flows into the Delaware, but much nigher in the days of Penn, the creek at that time extending its waters more westward. It stood, though in ruins, until nearly 1800, and its foundations were struck upon in excavating the cellar for the present building. Between Wade's house and the river, stood the ancient pines and walnuts, that waved a welcome to the peaceful footsteps of a commonwealth's founder. One of the walnuts yet remain, but the last of the pines was felled by a storm in 1846. A holly tree, which grew near the centre of where Penn and Front streets now intersect, likewise flourished in 1682, and was known, subsequently, as Penn's Holly; it died in 1859.

The *exact spot* of the landing is recognized as being near the south front of the residence of J. M. Broomall, Esq., about forty feet from the porch, and fifty feet eastward of the line of Penn street. Its locality is preserved by a Pine tree, planted under the auspices of Mr. Broomall and the Historical Society of Pennsylvania. This tree is the successor of the last venerable pine, and it is hoped that it may ong flourish upon and shade the consecrated spot.

FIRST PROVINCIAL ASSEMBLY.

Upon the 4th of December, of the year in which Penn landed, he convened at Chester the first Assembly that ever gave laws to the Province. It was composed of members of the Province, consisting of Bucks, Chester and Philadelphia counties, and for the three *lower counties*, New Castle, Kent and Sussex. The Assembly chose Nicholas Moore their chairman. An act of union was passed on the 7th of December, annexing the three lower counties to the Province, likewise a framework of government for the new commonwealth. The Dutch, Swedes and others who were deemed foreigners, were recognized as citizens, and laws which had been drawn up in England were passed upon. The meeting of the Assembly continued three days, having been characterized by harmony and candor. In this short period of time sixty-nine acts, or rather sections of an act, were passed, entitled "The great law, or body of laws, of the Province of Pennsylvania and the territories thereunto belonging.

In this act, provision is made for liberty of conscience, and the preservation of society from the various evils and crimes to which a people in the mass are subjected. None of its provisions is believed now to be in force. To those who are anxious to examine them, they can be found at length in Hazard's Annals of Pennsylvania, p. 619.

The *place* of meeting of this first legislative body in the Province, was subsequently known as the Old Assembly House. The building stood upon the west side of what is now Edgmont street, about one hundred and twenty feet north of Filbert, on ground now owned by Joshua P. & Wm. Eyre; it was removedin 1842. It was built of brick and used by the Friends as a place of worship from 1688 to 1736—the last use, previous to its demolition, to which it was devoted, was for the purpose of a Cooper's shop.

Having made Chester the original place of legislation, the people very sanguinely believed that Penn would make it the metropolis of his Commonwealth. For such a hope there were very substantial reasons. Here, the Delaware, with its wide reach of waters, its deep channel and bold shore, its interior country finely adapted to tillage, and with most eligible mill sites; its tall forests furnishing substantial material for structures; a picturesqueness that in time would give beauty to an extensive landscape; and a colony imbued, for the most part, with his own religious sentiments, already planted by the arts of peace, and vigorous sinews ready to build upand extend improvement, were circumstances, well calculated to weigh upon the mind of the benevolent commoner.

But there were other circumstances of a counteracting tendency that prevailed. Though not positively known, two, with propriety may be suggested. Previous to leaving Chester he deputed a commission consisting of Wm. Crispin, John Bezar and Nathaniel Allen, "to have the rivers and creeks, sounded on my side of the Delaware river, especially at Upland, in order to settle a great town, and be sure to make your choice where it is most navigable, high, dry and healthy; that is, where most ships may best ride, of deepest draft of water, if possible to load or unload at the bank or key side, without boating and lightering of it. It would do well if the creek coming into the river be navigable, at least for boats up into the country." Under these instructions the commission extended their examination up the Delaware, and returned with glowing accounts of the locality in that region. Upon visiting the spot where Philadelphia was afterwards located, it at once challenged the admiration of Penn and determined his purpose. It is true that Chester fulfilled his conditions to a very great extent, but the Schuylkill and the Delaware upon either side of his city, with corresponding advantages, seemed to fulfil them better. The other circumstance, likewise of geographical consideration, was in relation to a claim to territory conflicting with his own. Although he had by a formal act annexed to his province the "three lower counties," now forming the State of Delaware, and fully believed that his charter justly covered the country as far south as Cape Cornelius or Henlopen, he was aware that Calvert, Lord Baltimore, claimed territory to the 40th parallel of north latitude. Should he found a metropolis south of that line, and fail to establish a title against Calvert, great embarrassment and trouble must have ensued. It was of some consequence, therefore, that the disputed territory should be avoided. It may be observed, however, in relation to this matter, that Penn barely cleared his distance at Philadelphia, as the southern edge of the city, when Mason and Dixon were sent from England to adjust the boundaries between Pennsylvania and Maryland, was in latitude 39° 56′ 29.1″ north.

SEAT OF JUSTICE.—COURTS.

As the first settlement of Chester County, Chester, or Upland, early became the Seat of Justice, and the boundaries of its jurisdiction defined. During the temporary reversion of the South-River province to the Dutch, in 1673, the authorities at Manhattan empowered a majority of the inhabitants to name eight persons for each Court of Justice. These Courts consisted of "Justices of the Peace, whereof three to make a *coram*, and to have power of a Court of Sessions, and decide all matters under £20, without appeal, unless otherwise agreed among themselves. Above £20, and for crime extending to life, limb and banishment, to admit of appeal to Court of Assize." These Justices' courts were courts of record of an inferior grade, yet well adapted to the yet uncomplicated legal wants of an infant community. We hear of nothing definite relative to these courts until 1676, under Gov. Andros, for the jurisdiction of England, who ordered three courts to be held, one at New Castle, one at Upland and one at Whoorekills, and that the one at Upland begin upon the second Tuesday of each month.

With regard to Upland, we have the following, to us, very *intelligible* boundary, by which it will be seen that it was named, in its juridical powers, in 1678, as a county. "This county of Upland to begin from the north side of Oole Fransen's creek, otherwise called Steen-Kill, lying on the *bight* above the *Verdrietige Hoeck*, and from the said creek over to the single tree point on the east side of this river." This defines the boundary between Upland and New Castle, whilst the former ran as far northeast as the river Schuylkill. It must be observed that in speaking of the courts of Upland, we are not to suppose they were always held in the village of that name. In those more primitive days they were held at various places, to suit the convenience of the inhabitants, and very often in private houses. Thus in April, 1678, the court for Upland, was held at the house of Justice Peter Cock, on Schuylkill; and in March, 1681, "in the town of Kinsesse, Upland county;" we find, however, mention made of *court houses* in the first named year.

The clerks of these courts were to be approved by the Governor, and writs, and other law proceedings, were to be in the name of His Majesty, Charles II. The first record at Upland is of a court November 14, 1676, in which matters of both Church and State came within its jurisdiction. In 1677 "the Upland court was held at Niels Laerson's house; the expenses were one hundred guilders." The same year the court was ordered to levy for expenses of government, twenty-six guilders for each tyable," payable in wheat or other products of the soil: the number of tyables then reckoned in Upland jurisdiction being one hundred and thirty-six.

The first record of Chester County Courts at Upland is September 13, 1681. The Justices were Wm. Clayton, Wm. Warner, Robert Wade, Wm. Byles, Otto Ernest Cock, Robert Lucas, Lassey Cock. Swan Swanson, Andreas Bankson. Sheriff, John Test; Clerk, Thomas Revell.

The proceedings could not have been governed by very stringent rules of evidence, as we find that "Lassey Cock, upon proclamation in this court, that if any had anything against him, they should declare it; whereupon Daniel Brenson and Chs. Brigham, upon solemn attestation, declared that they heard certain Indians speak against him; the said L. Cock, upon oath, declared his innocence, and was thereupon cleared by the court." It is not probable that a declaration of innocence would go quite so far with a court in these rogueish times. In the February court, 1682, *Chester* is named for the first time upon its records. At the court held there in June, 1683, William Penn, the Proprietory, presided in person.

The first court under the Justices in West Chester, was held in 1786, in which year the Seat of Justice was removed from Chester, and the courts under their authority continued until 1791, when they presided for the last time. In the November term of that year the judges appointed under the Constitution of 1790 took their seats. From 1791 the President Judges have been,

William A. Atlee-----------from November, 1791.
Walter Finney---------------------------1793.
John J. Henry--------------from February, 1794.
John D. Coxe--------------------from May, 1800.
Wm. Tilghman ---------------from August, 1805.
Bird Wilson------------------from April, 1806.
John Ross-----------------from February, 1818.
Isaac Darlington----------------from July, 1821.
Thomas S. Bell-----------------from May, 1839.
John M. Foster (not confirmed) from December, 1846.
James Nill (not confirmed)--------from May, 1847.
Henry Chapman----------------from April, 1848.
Townsend Haines, elected under the Constitution of 1838, for ten years, from December, 1851.

REMOVAL OF SEAT OF JUSTICE.

The removal of the court from Upland was ordered in 1680, and Hazard states, that "Upland Creek, where the sessions of the court had heretofore been held, being at the lower end of the county, they resolved, 'for the greater ease of the people,' for the future to sit and meet at the town of Kinsesse, on the Schuylkill." This removal, however, was undoubtedly but temporary, and a part of the system of accommodation of that time, that justice should be had within convenient distances to all.

Chester was the Seat of Justice until 1786. Seated upon the southeastern edge of a widely extended district, those who lived westward became impatient of so long a travel to the county seat, and resolved to effect a removal to a more central position. In 1784 an Act of Assembly was procured for this purpose; West Chester, better known as the Turk's Head, was determined upon as the site, and public buildings were commenced under the active supervision of Col. Hannum. These proceedings were highly offensive to the people of Chester, who were jealous of what they deemed a prescriptive right to its long standing honors, and active preparations were made to counteract the proceedings of their more inland neighbors. By their exertions the repeal of the removal act was effected, and some of the citizens of the ancient bailiwick of Upland, who were determined upon a yet more vigorous measure, made preparation to march up and demolish the Court House in process of erection at West Chester.

A force, with a field piece, was rallied under Major Harper and marched upon the offending village. Arrived at the Gen. Green tavern, a few miles eastward of West Chester, the Major quartered for the night, resolving upon the ensuing day to effect the work of destruction. In the meantime, advised of Harper's movent, Col. Hannum, and some active confederates, made preparations during the night for the defence of the place. Arms and amunition, with proper quantities of whiskey and 'other refreshments,' were collected, loopholes for musketry made, and men concentrated in the court rooms.

Upon the ensuing morning Harper marshalled his force and planted his piece in the vicinity of an eminence, called Quaker Hill, which commanded the Court House, and prepared to batter the walls. At this juncture, however, some judicious persons got among Harper's men, and made such representations as induced a cessation of hostilities. Amicable relations were soon established, and the Major, after inspecting the defences, and firing his cannon by way of a peace rejoicing, made the Old Turk's Head the theatre of conviviality. A general jollification was an institution for a time, and the besiegers returned home quite mellowed by the refreshments of their hospitable host. Satisfied that no more overt acts would be made to resist a removal, the Court House was finished, and in 1786 another act of removal was procured, under which the transfer of the county government was peacefully consummated. Wm. Gibbons, then Sheriff of the county, removed the prisoners from the old jail at Chester the same year. Dr. Darlington characterized the old Court House of West Chester, a "miserable specimen of architecture," and he came very nigh the truth. No proceedings were instituted against Harper, the West Chester wags contenting themselves with newspaper squibs, quillets of wit, and lampoons couched in doggrel rhyme.

Fate takes hopeful revulsions; flattered by the sagacity of the unfortunate Uplanders, she once more turned a smiling face upon them. Thus, when there seemed to be a general acquiescence in the deprivation of the Seat of Justice, under which the public buildings were sold, the organization of the county of Delaware changed the current of events. The authorities repurchased the public buildings, and Chester, in 1789, suffering a lapse of but three years, found her ancient *regime* in a great measure restored.

The capricious goddess was not yet done with the well satisfied jurors of Chester; though they rejoiced in the restoration of their well sustained judicial honors, and enjoyed them from 1789 until 1851, a period of sixty-two years, the position of the Borough, yet too far eastward, was made anew, an argument against her. The agitation commenced, and in 1847 a law for the removal of the Seat of Justice having been put to vote at the October election of that year, the removalists carried the question by seven hundred majority. In 1851 the courts were removed to Media, and the first court was held the same year at the young metropolis.

But a shadow of hope for Chester grew out of a decision given by the Supreme Court of the State, relative to the License Law of 1847, which was declared unconstitutional, in consequence of having been put into operation by a vote of the people. The removalists, finding that the law authorizing removal had effect given it in a similar manner, and that the opposition thereto held it to be *ipso facto* void, endeavored to procure a remedial act, but were defeated in this movement by the activity of their opponents. The case was then taken to the Supreme Court, which in its wisdom found a distinction between the circumstances under which the people breathed life into the License Law, and those for the removal of the Seat of Justice; whereupon the latter was pronounced constitutional. This closed up the controversy forever upon removal, and Chester, having been the seat of judicial power for one hundred and fifty years, was forced to yield to the uncompromising demands of time: her ancient hall is destined to be trodden no more by the footsteps of the thronging multitude, who wait with patience upon the law's delay.

COURT HOUSES.

Different buildings at various times have been used in which to administer justice at Chester. The first we hear mentioned is in 1677, when "Capt. Jans Jurgin was ordered and desired by the Court to warn his men belonging to his company, and with them to fit up and finish the *house of defence at Upland* fit for the court to sit in, against the next court;" and in 1679, "Neils Laerson is ordered by court to make or leave a lane or street from Upland Creek to the house of defence or country house, before next court," which is the building referred to in the first order. This court house is supposed to have stood upon a lot upon the east side of Edgmont street, and nearly opposite the site of the Old Assembly House.

The sites of the first two can only be conjectured, and the site of the third, though known, contains but few remains for recognition. It is believed to have stood thirty feet south of the Old Assemby Building, and part of one of its walls is still standing as part of the wall of a dwelling owned by Frederic Fairlamb, Esq. The jail was in the cellar, and the bars of its windows are still in their original position. This court house was built by John Hoskins in 1695, and conveyed by him to the Commissioners of the county.

The fourth court house, a substantial stone structure two-stories high, was built in 1724, which date may be seen upon its south wall, and is in a good state of preservation. Its position is upon the west side of Market street, between Work and Free streets. The building contains the town clock, and its architecture denotes the olden time, being girded above each story with roofed projections. The jail, its necessary companion, stood upon the same lot at the corner of Market and Work streets, and its walls having been built upon, now resounds to the hum of machinery, having been merged into a manufactory of cotton goods. The front part, on Market street, which was the Sheriff's dwelling, may still be seen in pretty good preservation. The Court House will long stand, albeit one hundred and thirty-five years have driven their blasts against it, but the eloquent efforts of the forensic aspirant, is forever lost to its walls, its glory having departed by the removal of the seat of justice to Media. It is now used as a Town Hall, and opened for an indefinite variety of purposes; lectures, public meetings, balls, sales of furniture &c.

REVOLUTION.

In the summer of 1777, the invasion of Pennsylvania by the British forces became evident, and Washington directed the attention of Congress to the necessary means of defence. Chester and other counties of the State were called upon to forward their quota of men, and under the supervision of General Wayne a camp was formed at the village of Chester. Upon the 16th of August, 1000 troops were reported as having arrived at camp. As soon as a hurried discipline formed the concentrating masses into something like order and steadiness, batallions were organized by Gen. Armstrong and despatched upon the anticipated route of the enemy's approach. A letter from that officer dated Chester, August 29, 1777, states that 1800 men, worked out of the chaos of disorder into something of definite shape for military operations, were forwarded to Wilmington. This labor of recruiting and organizing went on until the eve of the battle of Brandywine.

During the 12th of September, the day subsequent to that disastrous conflict, Chester, from being the scene of the marshalling in arms, was pressed by the wearied footsteps of the defeated patriots, having been upon the line of retreat, and selected as a point upon which to rally for a renewed defence of Philadelphia. Unable to effect more than the bringing together his scattered batallions, Washington soon continued his march northward to be ready to cover any approach to that city; and a portion of Sir Wm. Howe's troops took possession of Chester. The occupation of the town continued virtually until the spring of 1778, when the British army evacuated all their posts in Pennsylvania.

During the Rebellion known as the Whiskey Insurrection in 1794, Chester sent a company of Infantry to the scene of disturbance, under the command of

Capt. Wm. Graham; and in the war of 1812 she furnished a company for Camp Dupont, under the command of Capt. Samuel Anderson.

ORGANIZATION OF DELAWARE COUNTY

Having lost the seat of Justice in 1786, the citizens in the eastern part of Chester county endeavored to secure the organization of a new county to be called Delaware. This was effected in 1789, the new county having been taken from Chester, and is the least of all the counties in dimensions. Its length is 16 miles, breadth 11; area 177 sq. miles. The population in 1790, 9,483; in 1800, 12,809; in 1810, 14,-734; in 1820, 14,810; in 1830, 17,323; in 1840, 19,-791; in 1850, 24,679.

EARLY SETTLERS AND LANDS.

The terms agreed upon by Penn whilst in Englanp in 1681, upon which settlers should possess land, was, "to those who buy, £100 for 5000 acres, free from any Indian incumbrance, and one shilling quit rent for 100 acres; to those who rent, one pence per acre, not to exceed 200 acres. For servants the master shall have 50 acres per head, and 50 acres to be given to every servant when his time is expired." For cities or towns 100 persons could have 50,000 acres surveyed and divided to suit their interests. In 1682 we find some modification of these terms. It became usual to grant 5000 acres to six purchasers, who chose land eligible for towns In this way, at Chester and other places lands were granted. For purposes of profit, in 1682, Penn granted to H. Moore and others, deeds for large bodies of land, and gave them a charter under the title of the Free Society of Traders, to whom extraordinary privileges were granted.

SWEDISH CHURCH.

Whether the Swedes ever had a church at Chester

may fairly be questioned. Says, Ferris "in 1681 the Swedes had three places of worship, one at Cranehook, near Christina, one at Tinicum and one at Wicaco." In regard to the erection of these we have definite dates, whilst no mention is made of Upland. They could have had no church edifice in 1675, as it was in that year ordered "that the church at Tinicum Island do continue as heretofore; that it serve for Upland and parts adjacent." Hazard in speaking of that period, says,—"it is probable there were at this time but three churches in the present Delaware and Pennsylvania."

"The Swedes," says Rev. Mr. Hall, "were Episcopal in their order of the Christian ministry, and held to liturgical service," and though he surmises that they may have erected a church in 1682, or as early as 1650 or 1660, he very properly evinces doubts upon that point. In the absence of positive testimony; from the fact that Tinicum church was but about three or four miles distant, and water communication convenient, and the evident impossibility of every author, who has written upon the Delaware settlements, failing to note the fact of a Swedish Church having been built at Upland, whilst at every other spot, however insignificent, the date of erection and their pastors are minutely given, we cannot avoid the conclusion, that, however apparent it may be to some minds, the Swedes never erected a church at Chester. They probably had a burial place, that now owned by the Episcopalians, corner of James and Welsh streets, whilst their place of worship was at Tinicum. It is altogether out of the question to suppose that Mr. Clay, a Swedish minister, in his annals of the Swedes, and which had particular reference to their religious interests on the Delaware, would have overlooked their interests at Upland.

FRIENDS.

Friends found their way up the Delaware in 1676, and settled in New Jersey. From thence families, having friendly intercourse with the Swedes, settled at Upland, Shackamaxon and other places. But there must have been arrivals at Upland previous to this, as another authority states that the Friends had meetings in their houses at Upland as early as 1675, in which year Robert Wade came out; and that they were visited by Wm. Edmundson, the same year, at Wade's house, where the first meeting was held. The first monthly meeting was held at Wade's on the 10th day of 11th month, 1681, and consisted of Friends of Upland and Chichester. It was called Chester Monthly Meeting, and grew large enough in 1696 to settle meetings at other places, from which sprung the meetings of Springfield, Providence and Middletown. The first meeting house of the society at Chester was the Old Assembly Building, purchased by them in 1688. They held this building until 1736; about that period the present house, on Market street south of James was built, and was the place of worship for the village and surrounding neighborhood, until the division of the sect in 1827. At that time, one party of the dissentients moved its place of worship to Waterville, where it has since continued its meetings, leaving the other in quiet possession of the house at Chester. Though the Friends were the prevailing sect in the surrounding country, at an early period, their number in the town was never great; and since 1827 they have very sensibly lessened. John Salkeld was a minister of some note among them in 1750.

EPISCOPALIANS.

The time at which the Episcopalians first associated together in Chester runs beyond any record which can now be found. In a notice by the Rev. Mr. Hall, he says:—"At this late period nothing can be determined on with respect to the precise time of the erection of the church edifice of St. Paul; we may however venture to say, that the probable date is somewhere about the year 1650 or 60, and that the Swedes were probably the first founders." Their record, extant, extends back to April 14th, 1704, at which time the congregation worshipped in the old edifice that stood in the burial ground directly opposite their present edifice. How long before that date they had occupied it is not known, but Mr. Hall's dates seem to be somewhat early. Whenever the time of building the original edifice, it is probable they were conjoined by the Swedes, who worshipped with them. The edifice was repaired in 1702, under the auspices of the "Society for the Propagation of the Gospel in England," and we find the Rev. Henry Nicholls was pastor in 1704. The ground upon which the first edifice was erected, was owned originally by James Sandelands, a merchant, and owning much property. The probability is that he gave them the ground, as it is stated that he was one of the founders of the church. Sandelands died in 1682, at the age of 56; so that if Mr. Hall's supposition, with regard to date, is correct, and Sandelands was one of the founders, it is possible that St. Paul may have been founded between 1660 and 1670.

In 1835 the church underwent repairs; the number of pews was increased, a new chancel built, a belfry erected upon the roof, with a bell, a gallery thrown across the west end of the building, and other improvements made in accordance with the wants of that time. In 1850 still further improvements were effected by the building of the present edifice upon the north side of James street. The style is Gothic, and of the most substantial character. It is built of stone, eighty-four by fourty-four feet, and appears as though an earthquake could hardly disturb its foundations.

The old structure, which stood upon the opposite side of the street, and had subserved the holier purposes of primitive days, then yielded to the fiat of time, and the stone that marked the grave of Sandelands, and a few other crumbling ones, are the only mementos of the spot, where

"The rude forefathers of the hamlet sleep."

The first edifice was small, having contained but twenty-four pews. Its style was very primitive; one of its gables was occupied by a large window, and exterior to the other was a tower some twelve feet distant from the gable, containing a belfry. The pulpit had its old fashioned sounding board. Among the venerable relics of olden time, which, by the courtesy of Dr. J. M. Allen, we were permitted to handle, are two chalices and their salvers, or plates; the one presented to the congregation by Queen Anne, the other by the Hon. Sir Jefferey Jeffries. The pieces are of very pure silver, but of workmanship somewhat rude, in comparison with the refined skill of our own time. The chalices bear the marks of the workman's hammer, and appear to have received their polish principally by long and frequent handling. The chalice presented by the Queen has engraven upon it *Annæ Reginæ.* The time at which these pieces were presented is not certainly known, but it must have been prior to 1702, as they were used at the first communion of the church. They are still regularly used.

There are some monumental remains in the church yard of dates subsequent to 1700, and should probably be noticed, under the present head. The oldest of these is inscribed as follows:

"Here lyeth ye Body of Charles Brooks
Who Dyed
(No date.)
Also Francis Brooks Who
Dyed August ye 9th 1704 Aged 50"

The next in date runs,—

"Robert French Obt. Sept. the 9th
1713"

This is cut upon an ordinary slab of sienite, six feet long and three and a half feet wide, and made the stepping stone from the front gateway of the present church edifice. The next we propose to notice, is in memory of

"Paul Jackson, he was the first who received a Degree in the College of Philadelphia—An. Æt. 38
A. D. 1767"

A tomb within the old church yard enclosure, contains reminiscences which cannot, with any degree of propriety, be passed by. The tomb of MORTON is an obelisk of marble, about nine feet in height, without any ornamental carvings or appendages but the arms of the State of Pennsylvania, encircled by laurel. The sides of the obelisk front precisely upon the four points of the compass. The inscription upon the west side, runs:

"Dedicated to the Memory of John Morton, a member of the first American Congress from the State of Pennsylvania, assembled in New York 1765, and of the next Congress assembled in Philadelphia in 1774, and various other public stations
Born A. D. 1724
Died April 1777"

Upon the East side:

"In voting by states upon the question of the Independence of the American Colonies, there was a tie until the vote of Pennsylvania was given, two members from which voted in the affirmative, and two in the negative. The tie continued until the vote of the last member, John Morton decided the promulgation of the glorious Diploma of American Freedom."

Upon the North side:

"John Morton being censured by some of his friends for his boldness in giving the casting vote for the Declaration of Independence, his prophetic spirit dictated from his death bed the following message to them:

"Tell them that they will live to see the hour when they shall acknowledge it to have been the most glorious service that I have ever rendered to my country,"

Upon the South side:

"In 1775 while Speaker of the Assembly of Pennsylvania, John Morton was reelected a Member of Congress, and in the ever memorable session of July 1776, he attended that august body for the last time, enshrining his name in the grateful remembrance of the American People, by signing the Declaration of Independence."

Among the most ancient remains of the spot, is the stone that commemorates the death of James Sandelands, merchant, which has been preserved with commendable care by St. Paul's congregation, by being placed against the eastern wall of the vestibule of their present edifice. It was taken from the old church when torn down in 1850; it formed the front part of Sandelands' pew, having been placed upon its edge. It was the oldest memento upon the ground, and at once massive and unique. The slab is a grey sand-stone, six feet high, four feet wide, and about six inches in thickness. Upon the face, near the edge, which is rounded, there extends entirely around the slab a raised surface, about two and a half inches wide and half an inch in relief. Upon this relieved border the date of Sandelands' death is cut, as also that of his wife. The style is quaint and runs as follows, commencing at one of the corners of the stone:

"Here lies interr–d the bodie of James Sandelands, marchant, in Upland, in Pensilvania, who departed this mortall life Aprile the 12 1682 aged 56 years, and his wife, Ann Sandelands."

Across the middle of the face of the stone, is a breadth of relief similar to that around the border, but four inches in width, upon which is alatininscription.

The relieved border, and the relief across the middle, of which we have spoken as containing the inscriptions, leave the remaining face of the stone equally divided into two depressions, each nearly three feet square. These squares have various insignia in bold relief. As these, in circumstantial detail would require too much space, and as a description would by no means convey an accurate idea of them, we beg leave to refer the curious in antiquarian research,to the tomb itself, or to an engraving of it made under the direction of the Historical Society of Pennsylvania. Sandelands, as his tombstone states, was a merchant, and man of wealth in the town, possessing in 1681 all the land between Chester and Ridley creeks for a mile inland. He was supposed to have been a Swede, but it is just as probable that he was a Scotchman.

The succession of Pastors of the Episcopal church from 1704, is enumerated as follows:—Rev. Messrs. Henry Nickolls, George Ross, John Humphreys, Richard Backhouse, Thomas Thompson, George Craig, James Conner, Joseph Turner, Levi Heath, Joshua Reece, William Pryce, Jacob M. Douglass, R. U. Morgan, John B. Clemson, R. D. Hall, M. R. Talbot, G. W. Ridgely, A. B. Hard, Mr. Quick, Mr. Balch, N. S. Harris, Daniel Kendig, M. R. Talbot.

METHODISTS.

Prior to 1832, no effective efforts had been made by this sect, their worshippers having been few in number. Occasional meetings were held in the Court House, and though some attempts were made towards the organization of a church, they did not succeed until that year. The faithful zeal, so characteristic of these people, enabled the congregation, under many difficulties, to erect a small edifice in 1834. From that period they grew encouragingly, and in 1846 their present place of worship was erected. A large congregation attest the result of their labors.

CATHOLICS.

The rapid influx of members of this persuasion, induced by the existing and prospective growth of Chester, necessitated the forming of a congregation, and the erection of a church edifice in 1842. The corner stone was laid on the 29th of September of that year, and on the 25th of June 1843, the house was dedicated, under the patronage of St. Michael, in the presence of a very large assembly. It is a stone structure, in the Gothic style, 72 by 42 feet, with a spire 100 feet high, surmounted by a gilt cross. The tower contains a finely toned bell, weighing 1000 lbs., which is rung thrice a day. To the church edifice has been added a sacristy 12 by 22 feet, and a room for a Sabbath School, 16 by 24 feet. A parsonage 34 feet square, and three stories high, was built on the church lot in 1854, and is the residence of the present pastor, the kindly Father Haviland.

PRESBYTERIANS.

The first sedulous efforts of the Presbyterians in Chester, are of comparatively recent date, and were commenced by the Rev. Jas. W. Dale, in the fall of 1850. He continued preaching in the Court House for more than a year, and thus laid the foundation for ulterior success. In 1852 the edifice in which the congregation now worships, was finished and dedicated; and by the indefatigable and zealous labors of Mr. Dale, a church was organized in 1853, with but 17 persons as members, and a Sabbath School of 30 scholars, with Mr. Robert Benedict as the ruling elder. For two years from the organization of the church, the Rev. J. O. Steadman, of Wilmington, N. C., was the stated supply. He was succeeded for two years more, by the Rev. Geo. Van Wyck, in the same capacity. The present pastor, the Rev. A. W. Sproull, entered upon his labors as the first regularly called pastor of the church in the summer of 1856, and was installed in September of that year. The church is now in a flourishing condition, and bids fair to be an instrument of great and extensive usefulness

BAPTISTS.

The Baptists as yet have no regular organization, but are laboring to form a congregation and build an edifice. In anticipation of this, J. P. Crozer has given for the purpose a very fine lot upon the northwest corner of Penn and Second streets. Upon this Mr. Benj. Gartside has built them a small, but neat edifice, which is used for prayer meetings and lectures. It is probable that not much time will have elapsed ere a respectable edifice will adorn the present vacant space, and a worthy congregation shed good influences around them.

ROADS.

The most ancient thoroughfare along the Delaware' was that from Philadelphia to New Castle, through Chester. That part of it from Chester to New Castle was early laid out and called the King's road; whilst the part that ran from Philadelphia to Chester, was laid out in the reign of Queen Anne and called the Queen's road. The entire route subsequently was called the King's Highway. This road was the same as the present one through Darby, and in locating it, a direct line would have taken it through Chester, north of where it was placed. It is stated that Jasper Yates, a person of property and influence, a son-in-law of James Sandelands, diverted it southward along what is now Market street, and again westward along James street, and over Chester creek upon a chain bridge. In this divergence he was supposed to have some pecuniary interest, as the road thus ran over, or contiguous to his property. Comments were freely bestowed upon Jasper's course, and some one, more bitter than others, remarked, that "God and Nature intended the road to cross directly across the creek, but the Devil and Jasper Yates took it where it was located." Jasper was living in 1701.

Filbert street and one between it and the river, were laid out previous to 1690. The now unknown street was eaten away by the tides of the river, and its site is covered with mud and reeds. Market and James streets, forming part of the King's Highway, as likewise Work, Free and Welsh, were laid out previous to 1725.

NEWSPAPERS.

The *Chester and Delaware County Federalist*, afterwards changed to the Village Record, published by Charles Miner, at West Chester, had the whole weekly newspaper circulation of Delaware county up to Nov. 8th, 1819; when the first number of the *Post Boy* was published at Chester, by Butler & Worthington. This was the first paper ever established in Delaware county. The size of the paper was 15½ by 9¼ inches, printed on 4 pages of 4 columns each, with large type. All the work on it, including editing and distributing over the county by post riders, was done by Mr. Worthington and Wm. W. Doyle, the latter then a small boy.

After publishing the *Post Boy* about six years, B. & W. sold out the establishment to Joseph M. G. Lescure, who enlarged the size of the paper, changed the title to the *Upland Union*, and continued it under that name until the year 1838; when it was purchased by Williams & Coates, who were succeeded by

Alexander Nesbit, and afterwards by Alèxander McKeever; by whom it was published until 1852, when, for want of patronage, it was discontinued. During most of this time the labor on the Union was performed by the sons of the editor, who were minors. The Post Boy and the Upland Union, were published as neutral papers until the Presidential contest of 1827, when Lescure, who was a Democrat, was charged by the Adams party with favoring the Jackson interest. Lescure quarrelled with Wm. Russell a resident of the Borough, and an ardent supporter of Adams, which induced him to purchase a press and materials and commence the publication of the *Weekly Visitor*, which was edited by Strange N. Palmer, who is now a Judge at Pottsville. From the establishment of the Visitor, the Union became a party paper, and was the organ of the Democratic party of the county until its discontinuance. After a few numbers of the Visitor were published, a disagreement took place between Russell and Palmer, and the establishment was purchased by 30 of the active members of the Adams' party, who called themselves National Republicans. Each of these gentlemen subscribed $20, and Mr. Palmer continued editor and publisher, until after the close of the Presidential campaign, when the paper passed into the hands of Thomas Eastman, who published it until the year 1832, when it was discontinued. During the time Eastman had charge of the paper, the first year the Anti-Masonic excitement arose, and E. inclining to favor that new party, a meeting of the owners was called, (termed by their political opponents the 30 Fathers,) which resulted in the leaders of the Anti-Masonic party purchasing the interests of those who were most dissatisfied with the course the editor had pursued.

Some time after the discontinuance of the publication of the Visitor, the materials were purchased and removed to Darby by Y. S. Walter, and on the 31st day of August 1833, he commenced the publication of the Delaware County Republican as the organ of the Whig party. In November 1841, Mr. Walter removed the establishment to Chester, where it has continued under his editorship and control, with increasing patronage, up to this time. It contains six times the matter of the Post Boy, the original paper of the county, and is published on the same terms upon which that paper was issued.

In the Gubernatorial contest of 1835, a split occurred in the Democratic party, one section advocating the election of Muhlenburg, and the other that of Geo. Wolf. The Upland Union, advocating the cause of the latter, the friends of the former established a paper called The Delaware county Democrat, which was published and edited by Caleb Pierce, but their candidate having been defeated, the paper was sold to Mr. Mooney, and in a few months after was discontinued for want of support.

In May 1850 S. E. Cohen commenced the publication of a monthly neutral paper under the title of the Chester Herald, which on the 13th of September of the same year, he changed to a weekly, and a few months after for want of patronage it was discontinued.

In October 1856, a paper under the title of the Upland Union and Delaware County Democrat, was commenced by J. G. Michelon, under the patronage of the Democratic party, but after issuing a few numbers it shared the fate of its predecessors.

During the years 1857–8, a small Literary paper was issued at irregular periods, called the Evening Star, by the Washington Literary Society, an association of young persons, formed for literary improvement.

About the year 1843 a small paper advocating the temperance cause, called the Chariot, was published by Flavill & Jackson, which was shortlived. During the year 1840, a small comic paper called the *Owl*, was published at irregular periods by unknown proprietors, and distributed gratuitously at night. It was edited with ability, and created considerable excitement among certain portions of the citizens of the Borough.

GENERAL HEALTH.

Chester, lying upon an alluvial strip, and washed by the tides of the Delaware, which carry off every source of miasma, is peculiarly exempt from those destructive diseases which render the lower levels objectionable as places of residence. The well water is somewhat impregnated with chalybeate and saline matter. and to these medicated qualities may be owing, in some measure, the avoidance of several forms of disease. A resort to Saratoga, or White Sulphur Springs, would be quite unnecessary to an inhabitant of the ancient bailiwick. The spring water is of the purest kind, and the superiority of Delaware county butter, sought for in the Philadelphia and Baltimore markets, is very much owing to the purity and coldness of this water.

Exceptional to the diseases upon water courses, Chester has very few, if any, agues or intermittent fevers; and bodily vigor and health are well attested by the oldest inhabitants, as well as visitors in large numbers. No process of acclimation is needed to keep a sound mind in a sound body, and none found to bear evidence of disease of miasmatic origin. In 1832 the Cholera swept over the town without a case, and other epidemics find no victims. Says the intelligent and observant Dr. Owen,—"We have no endemic disease, and our epidemics are few and of the mildest form of the prevailing malady. Fever is an element in the disease of man attendant upon almost every instance of aberration from health, even the slightest cold. But whatever its concomitants, it assumes the type and general character of an intermittent, remittent, or continuous fever. But these fevers are believed to be as few and mild here as upon any other inhabited section of the globe; and so well is this supported by experience, that where death occurs from fever, uncomplicated, our citizens are in the habit of suspecting something wrong in the treatment. Dysentery, one of the grave diseases of our climate, is scarcely known here, not averaging one case in two or three years. Bilious fever, too, so much dreaded, is extremely rare, occurring not oftener than Dysentery; and the Typhoid, so tedious, has not given us ten cases within the last ten years. Liver complaints, and bilious diseases generally, find no fitted soil at Chester.

"Within a few years the population of Chester has largely increased, and though the writer has had opportunities of observation, he cannot call to mind a solitary case of intermittent fever or chills, contracted by any of the new settlers; notwithstanding some of these, from employment and exposure, are made the most liable to disease. One family, with eight children, living most exposed to the influence of the river, and flattest land, has enjoyed uninterrupted good health over two years. Extending the inquiry along the shore below Chester, embracing therein one dozen farms, some of the houses of which are located on the bank of the river, and none from it a quarter of a mile, including family, numerous city boarders, laboring men in harvest, and servants, the amount of sickness, of every kind, at each of these farms, is not worth to the physician an average of $10 a year at the charge of $1 a visit. The largest and most celebrated boarding house in this section of country, situated near the river, two miles below Chester, every summer filled to overflowing, including a herd of little children, does not average $20 a year for medical aid. On the farm adjoining this, there have been but three cases of sickness within the last eight years; and a farm nearest the river, one mile and a half below Chester, has been exempt from disease for a number of years. At the largest, and best farm in the county, lying one mile above Chester, and about half that distance from the river, there has not been a case of sickness for eight years. Another large farm one quarter of a mile above this, has been blessed with uninterrupted good health for a still longer period. Leaving these more notable instances, and taking a general view of the inhabitants, it is no rare circumstance to find large families in this neighborhood, living one, two, and three consecutive years, without occasion for medical aid for disease; whilst there is no one place that can be given in illustration of much sickness. As localities differ in amount and kind of disease, so do the distinct races of men differ in their susceptibility to particular maladies, and to the influences of particular locations. Yet these different nations find at Chester, the same freedom from disease, and the same invigorating effects of our pure, bracing atmosphere, as others do. The Irish, with their strong affinity for agues and fevers, live here most exposed with comparative impunity."

Even at the period of the early settlements, when, from the uncultivated condition of the country, disease would be more frequent and virulent, the instances of longevity denote a healthy location. Of the robustness of the Swedes, Penn says, "as they are a people proper and strong of body, so they have fine children, and almost every house full. It is rare to find one of them without three or four boys, and as many girls; some, six, seven and eight sons; and I must do them that right, to say, I see few young men more sober and laborious." Mention is likewise made of Richard Buffington in 1739, who that year had assembled at his father's house, 115 of his father's proper descendants in the persons of children, grandchildren and great grandchildren. The father was then 85 years of age and his first born 60. Richard Buffington is said to have been the first one born of English parents in Pennsylvania—he was born in 1679.

TAVERNS.

The number of Taverns in Chester at an early date was much greater than at present. About the year 1790, says a venerable resident, almost every house of any size was an inn. Among the most prominent of these were the following:

The Inn of Sarah Gill stood upon the property now owned by Rebecca Brobson, on the north side of James street, west of Chester creek, extending to the creek. The proprietress married an Englishman named George Gill, who sided with his countrymen, and went with the English army to Halifax. George afterwards returning to Chester was imprisoned, but liberated by an act of pardon. This house has not been a tavern for the last fifty years, and is still the residence of the intelligent and kindly Mrs. Brobson. At the period in which the Inn flourished, the people of Chester made their own malt, and a malt house stood upon the same lot; this was a brick building, and in a dilapidated condition fifty years ago.

Valentine Weaver owned and kept the Inn now known as the National Hotel, at the northeast corner of James and Edgmont streets. This property was conveyed in 1750, by William Preston to Solon Hanley, as the "Blue Anchor Tavern." It was kept by Edward Engle until he died, about 1810, and subsequently by his widow, until 1832 or 1833. During the time of Mrs. Engle's proprietorship, it was the popular and fashionable hotel of the place. The house is now kept by Mr. George Wilson.

The Blue Ball Inn was kept in the brick building still standing upon the northeast corner of Market and

Filbert streets. The sign, a blue ball, was attached to the end of a pole that projected through a hole made in the wall of the house. Samuel Fairlamb was the keeper. No tavern has been kept there for fifty years. For a number of years it was the residence of Sarah Malin, the widow of Francis Malin. Mrs. Malin recently died there.

The Washington House, on Market street, was built by Auber Bevan, and kept as an Inn of some note by William Kerlin. Kerlin was succeeded by his son-in-law, Joseph Piper, who kept the house until he died. It is now owned and kept by John G. Dyer, whose kindness and gentlemanly bearing have deservedly won him many friends.

The Columbia Hotel, at the northeast corner of Market and Free streets, was kept by the widow Witheys, and said to have been in her day the best hotel in the United States. The proprietress was the widow of an English officer, who enjoyed a pension of sixty pounds sterling per annum. Mrs. W. became wealthy, and died at an advanced age. The house is now owned by Mrs. Elizabeth Appleby, and kept by her son, Mr. Francis Appleby.

In the building at the southwest corner of Market and Work streets, now occupied as a grocery by Mr. Minshall, a tavern was kept by James Pennell. James' house became noted by his keeping a tiger for exhibition, which attracted numerous visitors. Pennell subsequently removed to the Black Horse in Middletown, where he continued his exhibition. As he was one day experimenting with the animal, he fell a victim to its ferocity, having been caught by it and so severely lacerated as to cause his death. The property is now owned by F. J. Hinkson, Esq., and no tavern has been kept there within forty or fifty years.

The brick house in Edgmont street, north of James, upon the tan yard lot, was likewise a tavern, and kept by a person named Johnson. The same house is now occupied by Mr. J. S. Bell.

In the second house from the corner of Work street, on the east side of Market, was a hotel kept by John Scantling, an Irishman, and the resort of all the sons of the Emerald Isle. For a number of years, and up to about 1855, it was kept as a tavern by John Irwin and his son, Wm. Irwin.

A beer House, called the Globe, was once kept upon James street, below Market, by a man named Scott, but abandoned as a public house for nearly fifty years. It was burned down in 1830, and the site is now occupied by the Upland Buildings, owned by Samuel A. Price.

IMPROVEMENTS.

Chester, from its early settlement, grew at a very slow pace. Holm says of it in 1702, "Macoponaca, which is called Chester, was a bare place, without a fort, but there was some houses built there." Oldmixon says of it in 1708, that it had "one hundred houses." This would give a population of probably 500 persons. But by the census of 1820, a population of only 657 is given it, and in 1850 had increased to no more than 1667, making an increase of but about 1000 persons in thirty years, averaging about thirty-four per annum, and in one hundred and forty-two years but about eight persons per annum! From the last period the foundation of her prosperity became enlarged. Her venerable and antiquated appearance began to pass away. Where time and flame had done their work, antiquity was supersceded by modern structures, and but few years can elapse ere the appliances within and around her, must make her a city whose architectural taste, industrial energy, extended trade, and cotemporaneous intelligence, will make her a homestead at once pleasant and profitable, and a tyro in prophecy might readily hazard for her future a rapid enlargement of area.

Until the year 1849, hemmed in by farms, which the possessors did not seem willing to relinquish, but few improvements were made beyond the seeming exigencies of the small population. Though enterprise wished for outlet upon which to exercise its energies, the surrounding land owners did not recognize its claim to a wider scope. From 1839 to 1848, but very few houses were erected. Towards the last of February of the latter year, the store and dwelling of Preston Eyre, comprising all the northwest corner of Market Square, was burnt; and under the ownership of J. M. Broomall, the site was embellished by that gentleman, with fine stores, of ample dimensions. From this date others multiplied, and a stimulous seemed to have been given to building and trade. This was increased by some fortunate circumstances, the most prominent of which was the bringing into market some of the farms that had been a barrier to the growth of the ancient Borough.

One of these farms was part of the old Wade property, which, with some additional land, comprised sixty-four acres along the Delaware southwest of Chester creek. Mr. Broomall's enterprise, in conjunction with that of John P. Crozer, induced the purchase of this tract in 1849. Streets of ample width were laid out, and liberal inducements given to all who needed improved dwellings. By building and selling at cost, and in many instances advancing to those without capital three-fourths of the means necessary to build a dwelling, these gentlemen soon dotted the new purchase over with modernized habitations. In 1855 Mr. Broomall bought out the interest of Mr. Crozer, and has since pursued the same liberal policy to those in need of a home. Upon this purchase there have been built forty-four brick dwellings, two cotton factories, five cotton and wollen factories, one bleaching and finishing factory, one dyeing factory, one oil mill, one steam saw and planing mill, one sash and door factory, one large seminary, numerous shops, coal and wood yards, three ship yards, and six hundred and ten feet of wharfing, besides other improvements.

One year subsequent to this purchase, in 1850, John Larkin, Jr., bought part of the Cochran estate, lying towards the northeastern part of the Borough, and with the laudable spirit of improvement, vigorously addressed himself to the task of making a new and regularly built town. His policy, likewise, has been of a highly liberal character, by placing the price of lots on a scale so low as at once to enable those in moderate circumstances to buy, and induce the capitalist to seek liberal investments. The old race course, which was upon the property, where feats of agile horsemanship prevailed, and time, money and rough jests, were freely expended, is now the scene of the steady march of improvement. The hum of industry is heard instead of the sportsman's halloo, and the racer and his jockey are supplanted by the steam engine, and swiftly revolving machinery. When Mr. Larkin purchased this property it was in one enclosure, with one small stone house and a stable upon it. At this date it contains two hundred and sixty dwellings, four cotton mills, one machine shop and foundry, two brick yards, one steam sash, door and furniture factory, one market house, one boarding school, one coach maker and one smith shop, two public schools, Odd Fellow's Hall, one bakery, and ten stores.

In 1852 Messrs. F. & A. Wiggins, of New York, purchased the balance of the Cochran estate, lying north of Mr. Larkin's improvements, and having opened streets through the new purchase, facilities are afforded to those who wish to purchase eligible sites for homesteads. Of this Bishop Potter has purchased seventeen acres, upon which is the old mansion house of the Cochran's, where occasional hours are spent from the arduous field of ministerial labor.

MANUFACTURES.

The manufacturing interests of Chester have received their greatest impulse since 1848. In that year Mr. James Campbell, the most extensive manufacturer of cottons in the Borough, led the way. His mill was the old jail at the corner of Market and Work streets, to which additions were built to some extent along the latter street, to accommodate the various machinery. The same building is at present occupied by the enterprising Mr. Stephens, Mr. Campbell having removed to a more extensive site upon a fine avenue, Broad street, laid out by Mr. J. Larkin. Mr. Campbell has been followed by Messrs. Stephens, Blakely, Green, Eccles, Knowles, Leiper and Irwing, and the Gartsides, all of whom, by their industry and perseverance, bid fair to make Chester eminent in the interest in which they are engaged. So far as we have been able to approximate the real condition of the cotton and woolen manufactures, they may be condensed as follows:

No. of Operatives------------------------500.
" " Looms-----------------------------518.
" " Spindles-------------------------16260
" " Yards of fabric manufactured per
annum -------------------4,000,000.
Investments-------------------------$362,000.
Sales per annum----------------------$529,000.

The oldest foundry in Delaware county is located in Chester, having been established by Mr. Kitts, in 1836: it is now owned by Mr. Charles A. Weidner and worked by Weidner & Co., who are at present putting the works in thorough repair, preparatory to extensive business. In the same business, Lewis Miller, on Broad street, and Jacob Haycock, on Filbert street, are building up the same interest by the conquering power of steam, and human skill and industry.

CHESTER LIBRARY COMPANY.

The Chester Library Company was established in 1767. Early in that year, according to the records of the Library, "a number of the most considerable inhabitants of the Borough of Chester, having from Time to Time had in Consideration the good consequences that would result from the Erection of a public Library in the said Borough, for the promotion of useful Knowledge, did at length proceed to enter into Articles, for the forming themselves into a Company for that purpose, agreeable to which Article they met on the tenth day of May, Anno Domini 1767, in order to pay in the sum of money proposed to be advanced by each Member, and to elect and chuse proper Officers for the more effectual carrying their designs into Execution, at which Time were chose

Directors—Henry Hale Graham, Elisha Price, David Jackson, Thomas Moore.

Treasurer—Thomas Sharpless.

Secretary—Peter Steel."

The company commenced with 163 volumes.

The number of Books in the Library at present is about two thousand. Nearly all the standard works of the day are purchased annually, and the collection is perhaps equal to that of any other Library in any of the Boroughs, outside of the large cities. The present officers of the company are:

President—Joshua P. Eyre.

Directors—Alexander M. Wright, John O. Deshong, James Cochran, Frederick J. Hinkson and John H. Baker.

Treasurer—Job Rulon.

Secretary—Y. S. Walter.

MISCELLANEOUS.

ISLANDS.—The changes effected by depositions of land, consequent upon changes of currents, are sometimes quite extensive. Islands now exist where once flowed navigable water. A slight obstruction of the current, causing deposites behind it, forms the nucleous from which solid ground is afterwards made. The island now opposite Chester may not have been known to the earlier inhabitants, as also many other islands of the Delaware river.

WILLIAM PENN, in the explanation of his motives for settling his Province, says:—"I went thither to lay the foundation of a free colony for all mankind, more especially those of my own profession; not that I would lessen the civil liberties of others because of their persuasion, but screen and defend our own from any infringment on that account. The charter I granted was intended to shelter them against a violent or arbitrary government imposed upon us." When Penn visited Chester he was thirty-eight years old, largely endowed with benevolent purposes, and at an age which gave him the spirit and vigor to carry them out.

ROBERT WADE was distinguished among the Friends of 1675, and his hospitable mansion, the Essex House, was always open to members of every faith. He is said to have owned the land upon the southwest side of Chester, or Upland creek, for some distance. His name is often connected with both the business and religious interests of Upland, and in all the relations connected with the early community he bore a prominent part.

JAMES SANDELANDS is spoken of by the writers of annals as a "wealthy Swedish proprietor," at Upland, holding a large tract upon the northeast side of Chester creek, running one mile from the river. The evidence that he was a Swede does not appear, and it is quite as probable that he was a Scotchman. He was a member and liberal supporter of the Episcopal Church, giving it donations of land, when needed, and one of the most prominent in the establishment of the ancient church of St. Paul. From Sandelands and Wade, all the titles along the creek for some distance, are derived.

THE YATE'S or Logan House, was built by Jasper Yates, the son-in-law of Sandelands, in 1700, and afterwards came into the possession of the Logan family. It is built of brick, two stories in height, and yet remains a substantial structure. It stands upon the north side of Filbert street, above Edgmont, and previous to the erection of buildings upon the opposite side of the street, commanded a fine view of the Delaware. Its embellishment at the period of its erection, the roofed projection over the first story, is gone, but the evidences yet remain, though partially concealed by paint.

THE GRANARY, it is said, was also built by Yates, though some ascribe it to Sandelands. It was built in 1700, upon a somewhat extensive scale, having depositories for grain in the upper story, whilst the lower was used as a biscuit bakery, and at one period prosecuted a thriving business, receiving its supplies of grain from the country north of the town as far as Lancaster county. The building stood upon the west side of Edgmont street, and where Filbert street terminates; its site is now occupied by the Chester flour mill, conducted by Messrs. Bartram & Sharples.

THE PORTER HOUSE, so called from having been the residence of the gallant Commodore. It was built in 1721, by David Lloyd, a lawyer of education, who had been a Captain under Cromwell, but who afterwards became a Friend, and a leader in opposition to proprietory interests; he was somewhat noted as a refractory adherent, though "amiable in his social relations." The house stands a short distance east of Welsh street, and but a few rods from where the river swept its tides, ere the extensive area of marsh, now in front of it, was formed. The surroundings give evidence of having been, in earlier days, a spot the amenities of which made it attractive. The house was altered by Com. Porter, and a better style observed than in the original structure; but the fingers of time are evidently making havoc among its architecture. It is at present the residence of Dr. James J. Porter.

Original Grant.—The original grant for twelve hundred acres, to six inhabitants for the "town of Upland," was divided among the purchasers, and we find that the one-sixth part thereof, two hundred acres, belonging to Hans Juriansen Kien, was sold to his brother, Jonas J. Kien, in 1677; this lot "lying between the houses and lots of James Sanderling and Jurian Kien;" Jonas made the same over, at the same time, to John Test, merchant.

Assembly of 1682 at Chester was dissolved by William Penn in person; the Speaker was Nicholas Moore, a lawyer from England. It sat from the 4th until the 7th of December, or about three days altogether. The mass of the acts passed having been agreed upon in England, where they were properly digested, the time of the Assembly was thus economized.

Assembly Building.—An intelligent friend, from the examination that he has given this historical structure, is of the opinion that the room therein, which has been spoken of by writers as the one in which the Assembly sat, may have been the *front*, instead of the *back* room. The two parts of the building were constructed at different periods—the one next to the creek, was of brick, and the front, next to Edgmont street, was stone, and built, as is supposed, at a later date. But the front building bore evidence when taken down, of greater age than the other, was a more commodious structure, and better adapted to the purpose of the Assembly. The brick part bore evidence of having been subsequently added as a kitchen, having had an oven built within and forming part of the original wall. The timbers, too, were in a better state of preservation. History, however, has otherwise stated the case, giving priority of time to the brick structure, and that it was the veritable one in which the Assembly was held.

Swedish Houses.—The houses of the first settlers generally had but one room, with a low door, which required a stooping position to gain entrance. To admit light, holes, with sliding panels, were made—sometimes isinglass was used as a covering. The houses were built of logs, the chinks being filled with clay. The chimneys were of stone or clay, as was most convenient, with ovens beside them. These structures in time were superseded by brick, though rude in manufacture, many of them having a black glaze. These made a most durable and substantial wall.

Travelling.—The earliest inhabitants of Upland travelled mostly by water, this being an easier mode than through the forest. For this reason the Swedes generally settled upon water courses, that intercommunication between the settlements should be easily effected. As paths were opened, journeys were made on horse back, with pillions for females. Time's busy hand eventually made the broad highway, over which rolled the light and graceful carriage, with its spirited steeds—the same magician again waved his wand, and into life sprung the iron way, its swiftly rushing engine, defying resistance and space.

State of Society.—In early times the social feelings and hospitality of the citizens of Chester were well marked. Society, in its more primitive condition, forces its members upon a more general level, and interchanges of kindness become universal. Mrs. Logan's experience was that "the people were simple-hearted and affectionate. Little distinction of rank was known, but all were honest and kind." The same lady called the period of her youth in Chester, "the silver age." The writer of this can add his testimony, to the effect, that in a canvass of the Borough for the Directory of 1859, he was received with a uniform kindness by the citizens, and *in no one instance* received an insulting or unkind reply to the many inquiries he had to make. He states this as a significant fact, strongly indicative of the tone and temper of society.

FISH.—Chester, for many years, has been a profitable market for fish. In the Spring of the year the shad and herring fisheries yield their annual tribute, and are brought up Chester creek in boats, to supply the town and surrounding country. In 1683 it is stated that they were "exceedingly plentiful," and the early fishermen could take six hundred at a draught; they were proportionably cheap. Six rock fish could be bought for a shilling, six shad for the same, and oysters for two shillings a bushel.

MARKETS.—Meats and vegetables are not sold to any great extent in the open market houses at Chester; the *green* groceries furnishing almost every article necessary to the larder. The luscious melons and other fruits of Jersey, its sweet potatoes, &c., may be seen in their season in great profusion, and of the finest quality at these shops. The necessity for regular meat and vegetable markets upon specified days is not felt, as the citizens can purchase them at all hours of the day from the ample supplies of the grocer. This convenience is one of very great importance, and the custom of *constant supply* is worthy of support.

Gas and Water.—Gas was introduced into Chester in the year 1856, and the business stands of the Borough nightly attract the passer by and furnish a brilliant light for his way, in addition to the lamps upon the corners of the streets. The citizens not deeming their finances equal to the introduction of the other essential element, water, at the same time, light heralded the way, leaving water to follow in due time. Wells and pumps will probably ere long give place to the hydrant, and we may here mention that Mr. Samuel Eccles, at the corner of James and Franklin streets, has pioneered the way in a different mode of supplying water from that in ordinary use. During the year he has sunk an artesian well, for the supply of his manufactory; at from a depth of about seventy-five feet he has succeeded in obtaining an ample supply of pure water. The boring was easily effected, by steam power, in a very short time, through portions of primitive rock, not difficult to penetrate.

Stoppages were generally made at Chester, previous to and after Penn's arrival, by vessels bound to colonies higher up the Delaware, and the numbers that sometimes landed for a brief sojourn made the town a lively place. In 1682, quite an influx of visitors arrived, twenty-three ships having stopped there, making a population for the time that would have soon constituted a city, had the visitors made the place a permanent home. But the City of Brotherly Love seduced them to her shore.

Game.—Though the early inhabitants of Chester suffered the privations incident to a new colony, the abundance of game afforded them an abundant supply of provision. It is recorded that wild Pigeons came in clouds, and flew so low as to be knocked down with sticks. Wild Turkeys were exceedingly large and fat. The Indians furnished them to the Swedes at very low rates. A turkey weighing thirty pounds, sold for a shilling, deer at two shillings, and fish proportionably low. A letter by Mahlon Stacy says—"we have peaches by cart loads—the Indians bring us 7 or 8 fat bucks of a day—without rod or net we catch abundance of herrings after the Indian manner, in pinfolds—geese, ducks, pheasants, are plenty." Swans then abounded—oysters were abundant six inches in length. We do not hear of the more modern rail and reed birds, which now afford profit and pleasure to the sportsman in the fall season. These birds come in the early part of Autumn in large numbers, to feed upon the seed of the thickly growing reeds of the low shore and half formed islands of the Delaware. The seed in its milky state, is very nutritive, and the birds fatten upon it in a few days, affording a highly palatable food. They are hunted in boats when the tide is sufficiently high to push the craft through the reeds. One person, called a pusher, stands in the stern, and with a pole forces the boat forward, and secures the game for the sportsman, who stands in the bow loading and firing as fast as the objects appear. During the bird season numbers from Philadelphia and other places visit Chester, for the exciting sport thus afforded by the flowing river of the Lenape.

WHITFIELD.—This celebrated clergyman preached in Chester in 1739, to about 7,000 people, his fame as a speaker having aroused the country. He was accompanied to town by 150 horsemen. His commanding eloquence was the wonder of his time, and his voice had a winning tone, having been very sweet and possessing great power.

PORCHES.—In olden time the necessary appendage to the town dwelling was the porch at the front door. It was of cheap and simple construction, with a flooring upon which was a seat at each side of the door at right angles to the building. Very frequently a roofed projection, either supported by pillars, or without them, afforded protection from the weather. In the pleasant moonlight evenings the porch was often the spot where social greetings kept alive the strong kindly relations of the citizens. The friendly front porch is with the past, having been long superseded by the ample portico, or the more elaborate veranda.

FLOOD OF 1843, called the Lammas Flood, did immense damage upon the creeks of Delaware county. It occurred in August, the rain having commenced upon the fifth of that month. More than fifty bridges were swept from their foundations and carried off, and the courses of the creeks were scenes of melancholy desolation. Chester being at the confluence of two large streams suffered in the destruction of property. The railroad bridge and that upon James street were taken away, besides houses having but frail foundations. The loss to the county in bridges alone was estimated at $100,000, and the damage to mill seats was great beyond all precedent. So heavy was this extraordinary flood that the water rose one foot per minute, and according to some statements, six feet in five minutes, and twenty-three feet in two hours.

YELLOW FEVER.—During the prevalence of the Yellow Fever in Philadelphia, in 1798, numbers fled to Chester to escape the contagion, whilst others, carrying the disease with them, soon spread it over the town, causing the depopulation of entire houses, and some streets.

POPULATION.—The population of Chester cannot be accurately ascertained at the census periods, in consequence of the government failing to give the number of inhabitants in the borough distinct from those in the township. In 1820 it was estimated at 657; in 1830 at 848; in 1840 at 1,000; in 1850 at 1667; in 1859 at 4107.

NORMAL SCHOOL.—From the town maÿ be seen this Institution upon a commanding eminence, and it seems to be so identified with the interests of the place, though but a short distance from the Borough line, as to demand a notice. From a distance the beholder can readily recognise its noble front, looming upon his sight,two hundred feet in length and forty feet deep upon the wings. Upon each story a broad hall runs the entire length of the building, and its recitation rooms, library and lecture rooms, parlors, dormitories and eating room, denote the most complete and ample accommodations for two hundred students. It is built of the gneiss rock of the vicinity, and is at once a fine architectural pile, with artistic proportions and strong, massive appearance. The shrubbery and trees of the lawn around it, are not yet fully grown, but the observan eye can at once perceive that it must become one of the most beautiful and delightful spots that could attract the footsteps of the student, or challenge his veneratiou and regard. From the observatory upon the central building, the far distant hills of New Jersey can be viewed, rounded into the dark blue, hazy outline, so charming to the eye of the artist; whilst within a nearer view, the broad Delaware sweeps its gleaming currents until lost to the visitor, its bosom fanned by many a flowing sail. The entire scene is instinct with life and grandeur, and beams with all the fitful feelings of poetic delight.

This massive structure was erected a few years since, at a cost of fifty thousand dollars, by John P. Crozer; and it must ever be a most honorable monument, far above heroic blazonry, or the renown of battle fields, to the memory of its founder; not only by its power to defy for centuries the destructive years of time, but in the sending forth to the world those who shall mould the human mind for all the best purposes of life. Such a memorial of true usefulness will endure when all other renown will have oultived human applause; and the name of CROZER deservedly live as long as its stately walls endure.

This was the second institution built by Mr. Crozer; the Academy upon Second street, a very finely proportioned building of brick, capable of accommodating a large number of students, and being an embellishment to that quarter of the town, was erected by him several years previous to the Normal School. Mr. Crozer has done well for posterity.

INHABITANTS in Chester in 1682 were a mixed population, being Swedes, Welsh, Germans, Dutch and English. The Dutch and Swedes, who had pioneered the way and been kindly received by the Indians, in turn received the English with friendly regard. From this mixture of nationalites we have various names, some of them modified by after generations. Wade, Dunn, Markham, Pemberton, Moore, Yardley, Lloyd, Pusey, Chapman, Wood, Rhoades, Hall, Townsend, Gibbons, Bonsal, Sellers, and numerous others of the English; Stille, Bengston, Kempe, Rambo, Peterson, Cock, Svensson, Wihler, Kyn, Johannson, Van der Weer, Pehrsson, Longaker, Erickson, &c. of Dutch and Swedes. Svenson is now Swanson; Bonde, Bond; Bengston, Bankson; Nilsson, Nelson; Gostfson, Justice; Jonsson, Johnson; Soccom, Yocum; Wihler, Wheeler; Kyn, Keen; Van der Weer, Vandiver; Pehrsson, Pearson; Paulsson, Poulson; Longaker, Longacre; Lucasson, Lucas, &c.

LIST OF STREETS.

The compiler of the Directory that follows, has taken a liberty, with regard to the names of some of the streets, which, for a stranger, may seem unwarrantable. He has not done so, however, without the approbation and advice of some responsible citizens, and the change of Front to Edgmont street, and part of the Darby Plank Road, to Free street, he thinks will at once appear reasonable and satisfactory. The change of Work street to Clinton, was likewise urged upon him, but as this change, by corporate authority, did not seem so evident, he did not feel warranted in assuming such a responsibility. The terms *above* and *below* are used in reference to the Delaware river. In those streets running parallel to Market, *below* is in going towards, and *above* from the river. In those streets running parallel to James, *below* is down and *above* up the river.

Bevan's Court, from Filbert N between Market and Welsh.

Barclay street, from Railroad to Fifth street, E of Concord road.

Broad street, from Edgmont to Darby P Road, N of Larkin.

Cochran street, from Upland to Plank Road, N of Railroad.

Courtland street, from Potter eastward, N of Prospect Avenue.

Crosby street, from Plank Road to Porter, East of Welsh.

Concord street, from Railroad, N to Borough line.

Clinton street, from Welsh to Crosby, S of Free.
Deshong street, from Potter to Borough line, North of Courtland.
Essex street, from James to Delaware river, West of Penn.
Edgmont street, from Delaware river to Borough line, W of Market.
Evans street, from Welsh to Crosby, S of James.
Filbert street, from Welsh to Chester creek, South of James.
Free street, from Edgmont to Railroad, S of Railroad.
Frederick street, from Edgmont to Potter, N of Gallatin.
Franklin street, from Fifth to Delaware river, W. of Essex.
Front street, from Penn westward, S of Second.
Fourth street, from Concord Road westward, S of Fifth.
Fifth street, from Washington westward, S of Sixth.
Fulton street, from Fifth to Water, W of Franklin.
Gallatin street, from Edgmont to Upland, N of Logan.
Graham street, from Market to Edgmont, S of James.
James street, from Crosby to Borough line, S of Fourth and Work.
Jefferson street, from Providence Road east, North of Franklin.
Larkin street, from Edgmont to Darby Plank road, N of Cochran.
Liberty street, from Edgmont to Darby Plank road, S of Logan.
Logan street, from Edgmont to Quarry, N of Liberty.
Morton street, from Providence road. to Potter, N of Frederick.
Madison street, from Free to Logan, W of Upland.
Mechanic street, from Larkin to Liberty, W of Madison.
Market street, from Railroad to Delaware river.
North street, from Railroad to Cochran, E of Upland.

Parker street, from Fifth to Water, W of Fulton.
Penn street, from James to Del. river, W of Chester creek.
Potter street, from Cochran to Providence road, E of Upland.
Providence Road, from Edgmont to Borough line, N E of Edgmont.
Prospect Avenue, from Potter east, S of Courtland.
Porter street, from Welsh to Crosby, S of Evans.
Powell's Court, from Market east, between James & Filbert.
Plank Road, from Railroad North to Borough line, E of North, Potter and Quarry.
Quarry street, from Broad north, E of Potter.
Rail Road street, from Edgmont to Darby Plank road, N of Railroad.
Second street, from Chester creek west, S of James.
Sixth street, from Concord road to Wade, S of Railroad.
Upland street, from Railroad to Providence road, E of Madison.
Work street, from Edgmont to Welsh, N of James.
Water street, from Fulton to Parker, S of Front.
Washington street, from Railroad to Fifth east of Barclay.
Walnut street, from Prospect Avenue to Borough line, E of Potter.
Welsh street, from Edgmont to Delaware river, E of Market.
Wade street, from Railroad to Sixth, E of Washington.
Washington street, from Railroad south, E of Barclay.

NAMES OF INHABITANTS.

ABBREVIATIONS.

Ab. above; bel. below; carpt. carpenter; gent· gentleman; lab. laborer; gentw. gentlewoman; manuf. manufacturer; merch. merchant; R. R. rail road; wid. widow; col. colored; cord. cordwainer; prop. proprietor; cor. corner; print. printer; lumb. lumber; cab. mak. cabinet maker; att'y attorney; wat. waterman; operat. operative; opp. opposite;

A

Abbot William, operat, Liberty bel Upland
Abbot David, saddler, James ab Edgmont.
Abbot Susan, confectionery, James ab Edgmont
Abbot Henry, ostler, James ab Edgmont
Abel Elizabeth, col wid, Bevan's Court
Abel Simon, col lab, do do
Ainsworth William, engineer, Second bel Fulton
Allen Perry, col lab, Welsh bel James
Allen Dr. J. M., Work ab Market
Allen Thomas, bricklayer, Essex bel Second
Allen H. T., sash maker, James ab Franklin
Amer John, moulder, Edgmont bel R R
Anstey Henry, cordw, Darby R ab R R
Anderson Sarah, wid, Broad bel Upland
Andrews Edward, lab, cor Filbert & Edgmont
Anderson Jas., grocery & flour store, James bel Market
Appleby Thomas, prop Columbia Hotel, cor Market & Free
Armstrong Thomas, operat, Welsh bel R R

Arnold Walter J., printer, Market & Powell's Court
Armitage Anna, wid, Second bel Fulton
Arthur Andrew, operat, Mechanic ab Broad
Armstrong John, plasterer, Madison bel Liberty
Ashton Robert, lab, Fulton bel Second
Atkinson John, tailor, cor Broad & Upland

B

Bagshaw William, moulder, Larkin ab Potter
Bailey Mr., engineer, Broad ab Mechanic
Baker & Eyre, lumber, coal & brick yard Edgmont bel James
Baker George & Co., dry goods, grocery & hardware, S E cor Market Square
Baker George, merchant N E cor Market Square
Baker John, carpt, Welsh ab R R
Baker Perciphor, lumb merch, Welsh ab R R
Baker & Eyre, brick yard, back of James ab Fulton
Baldruff Fred., confectioner, Free ab Market
Baldwin W., plasterer, Filbert bel Welsh
Barnard Thomas D., gent, Edgmont ab Work
Bartram & Sharpless, Chester flour mills, cor Edgmont & Filbert
Bartwell Daniel, confectioner, cor Broad & Upland
Barrowclough Joseph, tanner, Free ab Edgmont
Barker Joe, pattern maker, Broad ab Mechanic
Bardsley Samuel, operat, Liberty bel Quarry
Batchel Anthony, tin smith, Free ab Welsh
Baum Oley, ship carpt, Front bel Fulton
Bazely James, operat, Larkin ab Edgmont
Beale Lieut. Edward, U S N, Edgmont ab R R
Beatty John E., carpt, Second bel Fulton
Beaumont Joshua, photographer, Market bel Work
Beaumont Francis, oyster saloon, Market bel James
Bell John, operat, Second bel Fulton
Bell J. S., tanner, Edgmont ab James
Benedict Clarissa, wid, Potter ab Morton
Berry Alice, col. wid, Liberty ab Edgmont

Berry Washington, farmer, James bel Fulton
Berry William, dyer, Market ab Filbert
Bickley M. H., druggist, cor Market & Work
Birchell Lydia, gentw, James bel Market
Birtwell Daniel, baker & confecr, Market bel Work
Bird Amos, lab, Broad ab Edgmont
Bird Anna M., operat, Broad ab Edgmont
Bird Christiana, operat, Broad ab Edgmont
Biggerstaff John, tinman, Work ab Edgmont
Biggins Michael, tailor, Work ab Market
Bladen Dr. W. T., cor Edgmont & Free
Blakely Abm., Arasapha mills, cor Liberty & Quarry
Blakely Abm., manuf, cor Broad & Upland
Blakely Benjamin, manuf, do do do
Blakely Joseph, operat, Broad ab Upland
Blakely Reuben, manager, cor Potter & Liberty
Blagg Ann, wid, Second bel Essex
Blizzard William, lab, Upland bel Cochran
Boner Ann, wid, Darby R bel Liberty
Boner Mary, operat, cor Free & R R
Boon Peter, ship carpt, Filbert ab Market
Booth William, planing mill, Front & Essex
Booth John, carpt, James ab Essex
Booth Joseph, wat, Market ab Filbert
Booth Levin, wat, Edgmont bel Filbert
Booth John, gent, cor Edgmont & James
Booth William, wat, cor Market & Filbert
Booth Parker, wat, Market ab Filbert
Booth Henry, gardener, Liberty ab Potter
Booten, Wm., lab, Upland bel Cochran
Borden Wm., tobacconist, Market bel Free
Bottomly Geo., operat, Upland bel Larkin
Bowers John, operat, Madison bel Liberty
Bowker T. W., gas fitter, plumber, stoves, etc, cor Market & James
Bowers Joseph, cab maker, Madison bel Liberty
Boyle Emanuel, lab, Broad ab Edgmont
Boyle Charles, carter, Second bel Fulton

Boyle John, operat, North bel Cochran
Braden Leonard, carpt, Edgmont ab Providence R
Bradley Henry, lab, Market ab Filbert
Bramall Frank, operat, Fulton bel Second
Bramall John, operat, Front bel Fulton
Branton Howard, col lab, Welsh ab Filbert
Brandis H., clothier, Market ab James
Branson David, carpt, Front ab Essex
Brewster John, operat, Potter ab Broad
Brewster Wm., operat, do do
Brensinger George, teacher, Free ab Welsh
Bridges Emerson, machinist, Madison bel Liberty
Brierly Emanuel, cordw, Broad bel Mechanic
Brierly Thomas, shoe store, do do do
Brister Ellis, col cordw, Welsh bel James
Brobson Rebecca, wid, James ab Penn
Brogan Samuel, carpt, Front bel Penn
Brogan Edward, carpt, Larkin ab Edgmont
Brooks John, saddler, James bel Penn
Brooks Wm., operat, Front bel Fulton
Brooks John, saddler, Market ab James
Broomall John M., attorney, Penn & Delaware river
Brown Benjamin, engineer, cor Penn & Front
Brown Richard, wat, Welsh bel James
Brown George, col lab, Welsh bel James
Brown Samuel, lab, Concord opp Fifth
Brown Wm., bricklayer, Essex bel Second
Brown Henry, cab maker, Mechanic bel Liberty
Brown Thomas, operat, Madison ab Broad
Brown Sarah, wid, Edgmont bel Filbert
Bucha B. F., sash maker, cor Essex & Second
Buck Charity, wid, Franklin ab James
Buck James, cordw, Edgmont ab Providence R
Buckley John, bottler, Madison ab Broad
Buggy Robert, gent, Broad ab Upland
Bundy Benah, cordw, Essex ab Front
Bunce Thomas, lab, Front bel Parker
Bunce Patrick, cordw, do do do

Bunce James, lab, Second bel Parker
Burke Wm., operat, Work ab Edgmont
Burke Samuel, lab, Broad bel Upland
Burke Edmund, operat, Liberty bel Upland
Burke Joseph, lab, Edgmont ab Logan
Burke J. M., operat, Broad ab Upland
Burns Margaret, dry goods, cor Essex & Second
Burns George, cordw, Welsh ab R R
Burns Morris, boiler maker, Free ab Market
Burns James, cordw, Work bel Market
Butler John, operat, Upland bel Liberty

C

Caldwell John, Edgmont ab Providence R
Callahan Edward, quarryman, Mechanic bel Liberty
Calvin John, col wat, Free below R R
Campbell James, lab, Larkin ab Upland
Campbell Joseph, operat, Madison bel Liberty
Campbell James, manuf, Broad & Mechanic
Cantwell Mary, wid, Filbert bel Welsh
Carson Perry, col lab, Welsh ab Filbert
Carr Francis, lab, Darby R bel Cochran
Casha Draper, col seaman, Bevan's Court
Chadwick James, groc & prov, cor James & Edgmont
Chalfant Jacob, carpt, Work above Market
Chriswagoner George, brick mkr, Upland bel Liberty
Christer Wm., ostler, Washington Hotel, Market
Chipman Simon, col wat, Welsh bel James
Clark George, confectioner, Market near Filbert
Clark Dennis, baker, Market ab James
Clark Wm., gent, Edgmont ab Providence R
Clayton Charles, cordw, Work bel Market
Clayton Samuel, wat, Filbert ab Market
Clayton James, quarryman, Darby R ab R R
Clayton Joshua, lab, James bel Fulton
Clark John, lab, Upland bel Liberty
Cloud Stephen, Jr., boots, shoes and findings, James bel Market

Cloud Lewis T., cordw, James bel Market
Cloud Charles, cordw, Edgmont ab Liberty
Cloud James, ship carpt, Front ab Essex
Clyde Henrietta, gentw, Free ab Market
Coates J. R. T., att'y, Clinton ab Welsh
Coates Dr. I. T., Clinton ab Welsh
Coates Annie E., teacher, Clinton ab Welsh
Coates Lydia, wid, do do do
Coburn Wm., blacksmith, Upland ab Logan
Cochran J. E., gent, Clinton bel Crosby
Cochran John, real estate agent Market ab James
Cochran James, drover, cor Clinton & Crosby
Cohen Annie, operat, James ab Franklin
Collett Mary A., wid, Edgmont bel Filbert
Collins David, carpt, Market ab Filbert
Collins Charles, wat, North bel Cochran
Collins Daniel, cordw, Darby R ab Broad
Collison Peter, gent, cor Filbert & Edgmont
Collison Isaac, cordw, Filbert ab Edgmont
Colwell James, col lab, Welsh bel James
Congleton Edward, carpt, James ab Franklin
Conliff John, engineer, Darby R ab Broad
Conly John, lab, Market near Powell's Court
Cook Rebecca, col laundress, Bevan's Court
Coombe Sarah P., gentw, Edgmont ab Filbert
Coppoch Abner, cordw, Edgmont, bel R R
Coppoch Wm., plasterer, James bel Franklin
Coulter Mary, teacher, Broad ab Upland
Cowden Wm., operat, Work bel Welsh
Craig Wm., plasterer, Free bel Upland
Creighton John, lab, do do do
Crook John, weaver, Welsh bel Edgmont
Crowder Isaiah, Market ab Filbert
Crosson Amanda, wid, Welsh bel R R
Crosson Wm., quarryman, Darby R by Ridley creek
Culin Jacob, lab, Work bel Market
Cullion Michael, lab, Quarry ab Broad

Cunningham James, lab, Upland bel Cochran
Curry Wm., wat, James ab Fulton
Cutler Wm., F., machinist, James ab Welsh

D

Danford John, pedlar, Darby R ab R R
Darrah Ann H., gentw, Free bel Welsh
Darrah Susan, gentw, Free bel Welsh
Davis Mary, gentw, Free bel Upland
Davis Amos, plasterer, James ab Penn
Davis Hannah, gentw, Free bel Upland
Davis Benjamin, printer, cor Market & Powell's court
Denton Anna, gentw, Free bel Welsh
Deshong Alfred, gent, Edgmont opp Liberty
Deshong John O., gent, Edgmont opp Liberty
Devers J. A., grocery & prov store, Market bel James
Devolue Samuel, ostler, Powell's Court
Dickerson Asbury, wat, Powell's court
Dickinson S. A., wid, Providence R
Dickerson Wm., bricklayer, James ab Franklin
Dobbins J. W., carp, Work ab Edgmont
Dobbins W. K., carp, Work ab Edgmont
Donaldson John, operat, James ab Essex
Donaldson Henry L., teacher, Broad & Darby R
Donaldson Thomas, operat, Upland bel Liberty
Dolan Patrick, mason, Logan bel Upland
Dolan John, North bel Cochran
Dolan James, mason, North bel Cochran
Dougherty James, lab, Railroad ab Upland
Dougherty Barney, lab, Railroad ab Upland
Dougherty John B., wat, Edgmont bel Liberty
Dougherty John, lab, Liberty ab Potter
Dougherty Philip, pedlar, Liberty ab Darby R
Dougherty James, brickmaker, Darby R ab Liberty
Dougherty John, wat, Edgmont ab Filbert
Dougherty James, lab, Larkin ab Edgmont
Dougherty John M., watchman, Edgmont bel Railroad
Dougherty John, lab, James ab Fulton

Dougherty Michael, gardener, James bel Fulton
Dougherty James, wat, Franklin ab James
Downs John, col lab, Bevan's Court
Doyle L. C., millenery & trimmings, Market ab James
Doyle Martha, operat, Work ab Market
Doyle Wm. W., house & sign painter, Welsh ab R R
Dubois B. F., watch maker, Market bel Work
Dumont John, operat, Edgmont ab Logan
Durborow Charles, wat, Edgmont ab Filbert
Duffee Eveline C., dressmaker, Broad bel Upland
Duffy John, lab, Second bel Fulton
Duffy John, lab, Madison bel Liberty
Dunkerley James, machinist, Liberty bel Quarry
Durkin John, lab, Mechanic below Liberty
Dutton Samuel, shipcarpt, Second bel Essex
Dutton Jesse, carpt, James bel Penn
Dutton William, cord, James bel Penn
Dutton Aaron L., grocery & provision, Market ab James
Dutton R. R., lumb merch, Free ab Welsh
Dutton Caroline, saleswoman, Free ab Market
Dutton James, bricklayer, Filbert ab Market
Dyer John G., prop, Washington House, James opp Court House
Dyer Joshua, clerk, cor Front and James
Dyer Samuel, Washington House, Market st
Dyson John, operat, Mechanic bel Liberty

E

Eccles Samuel, manuf, cor James & Franklin
Edwards Mary A., wid, Edgmont ab Railroad
Edwards Geo., lab, Edgmont ab Providence R
Edwards Thos., operat, Front bel Fulton
Elliott Eliz., operat, Fifth ab Concord
Elliott Diana, operat, Work ab Edgmont
Ellam Geo., tailor, cor Broad & Upland
Emery Sol, col lab, Free ab Upland
Engle Mary, wid, Edgmont ab R R

Entwisle Joseph, bleacher, Penn bel James
Entwisle & Hall, bleachers, cor Front & Fulton
Enos Geo., wat, cor Market & Filbert
Esrey Elizabeth T., wid, Welsh ab R R
Evans Cadwalader, machinest, James bel Market
Evans Abbey A., gentw, James bel Market
Ewing Wm., lab, Darby R ab Liberty
Ewit Susan, col wid, Bevan's Court
Ewing Wm., lab, cor Market & Filbert
Ewing Jane, wid, Free ab Edgmont
Ewing Joanna, grocery, Filbert ab Market
Ewing Hannah, gentw, Penn bel James
Eyre Preston I., gent, Edgmont ab James
Eyre Sarah, gentw, Edgmont ab James
Eyre Jane, gentw, Edgmont ab James
Eyre Elizabeth, gentw, Edgmont ab James
Eyre Joshua P., farmer, Edgmont op Free
Eyre Wm., Jr., farmer, Edgmont op Free
Eyre Joshua P. Jr., merch, Edgmont op Free

F

Fairlamb N. W., cab mak & undertaker, Market bel R R
Fairlamb Frederick, magistrate, James & Crosby
Faith Chas. C., oyster saloon, Market & Powell's court
Faraday Martin, lab, Front bel Fulton
Fawley Annie, grocery & confec, James bel Market
Fawley Thos. K., gent, James bel Market
Fawley Samuel, operat, James bel Market
Feney John, lab, Market bel Powell's court
Feely Thomas, lab Quarry bel Liberty
Ferguson Wm., carpt, Penn bel James
Ferguson Mrs. A., milliner, Penn bel James
Field Frank, merch, Potter ab Morton
Fields Geo., col lab, Welsh bel James
Fields Basil, col lab, Welsh bel James
Fields Benj., col brickmaker, ab R R
Finch L. E., dry goods, James bel Market

Flavill Wm. H., surveyor, build & conveyancer, Free ab Welsh
Flavill Jane, milliner, Market near Town Hall
Flavill Edwin E., carpt, Free ab Welsh
Flood Geo., tobacconist, Edgmont ab Providence R
Fogg Robert, operat, Quarry bel Liberty
Forwood Dr. J. L., James ab Edgmont
Ford Benj., blacksmith, Filbert bel Market
Foster Thos., moulder, Edgmont bel R R
Fox Chas., carpt, Work ab Edgmont
Fox David, operat, Work bel Market
Fox Martha, operat, Work bel Market
Fox John, tobacconist, Franklin ab James
Franklin Lewis, carter, Liberty bel Upland
Freiger Constantine, cord, Fulton bel Second
Fricker Jacob, barber, Market bel James
Fuller Joseph, lab, Work ab Edgmont

G

Gaines Mary, col, Bevan's court
Gallagher John, lab, Concord op Fifth
Gallagher Jesse, cord, Liberty bel Quarry
Gallagher Neal, cord, Market bel R R
Garrett D. M., merch, James & Penn
Garside John, machinist, Upland ab Broad
Gartside Robt., plumber, gasfitter, hard, Penn Square
Gartside Benj., manuf. Fulton & Water
Gartside James, manuf, Second ab Fulton
Gartside Amos, manuf, Second ab Fulton
Gartside John, manuf, Fifth ab Concord
Garthwaite James, operat, Front bel Fulton
Gardner James, porter, Front & James
Geig Isabella, wid, Welsh ab Free
Gelston John, gent, James ab Welsh
Gelston Mary, operat, James ab Welsh
Gelston Sarah, operat, James ab Welsh
Gibson Humphrey, farmer, Concord ab R R
Gilpatrick Francis, lab, North ab R R

Glasgow I., col lab, Welsh ab Filbert
Glancy Daniel, dyer, James ab Edgmont
Gleason Timothy, lab, Welsh bel Edgmont
Glennon Edward, lab, Logan ab Edgmont
Glutzbeck Geo., cord, Filbert bel Welsh
Goddard Uriah, operat, Potter ab Broad
Goff Mary A., Steamboat Hotel, Market bel Filbert
Graham Dr. F. Ridgely, Free & Welsh
Grantham Jas., farmer, James bel Welsh
Grant Jona., operat, Front bel Fulton
Gray Dr. Wm., Market & Free
Gray W. C., dry goods & groceries, Edgmont and James
Gray Chas., blacksmith, James bel Penn
Gray H. B., blacksmith, James bel Penn
Greig John, books & stationary, Market ab James
Green Mrs., wid, Cochran bel Darby R
Green Wm. F., carpt, Work ab Market
Green Thos., apothecary, Market & Work
Green John, manuf, Edgmont bel Logan
Green John J., manuf, Liberty & Madison
Greenwood Jas., grocery, Welsh & R R
Greenwood Wm., bottler, Cochran & Darby R
Greenwood Stephen, operat, Logan ab Potter
Greenwood John, operat, Logan ab Potter
Griffin Daniel, lab, Upland bel Cochran
Grounsel John, blacksmith, James bel Franklin
Groves Joseph, lime & plaster, Market & Del R
Grubb Wm., wat, Edgmont bel Filbert
Grubb H. B., grocery & provisions, James bel Market
Grubb Wm. L., carpt, Second & Fulton

H

Haggerty Barney, stone cutter, Larkin ab Potter
Hall Charles, carpt, Larkin ab Upland
Hall Joseph A., carpt, Broad bel Darby R
Hall Charles W., operat, James bel Franklin
Hall John, bleacher, Second & Franklin

Hampson James, stoves and furniture, Market & Free
Hamilton Robert, lab, Edgmont ab Providence R
Hannum R. E., att'y, office Market ab Work
Hansel Mary, wid, Liberty bel Quarry
Hanley John, Robin Hood Rest, James bel Front
Hanvas Sarah, wid, Liberty ab Madison
Hard Rev. A. B , Potter ab Morton
Hardy Phineas, weaver, Edgmont bel R R
Harden Matthew, engineer, Mechanic bel Liberty
Harden John, operat, Frcnt bel Fulton
Hargraves Thomas, operat, Second bel Fulton
Hargraves George, operat, James bel Fulton
Harper Alex., carpt, Edgmont ab Liberty
Harper Catharine, wid, Second bel Fulton
Harper George, operat, do do do
Harris George, col lab, Bevan's Court
Hart Wm., manuf, Second & Franklin
Hart Alfred, operat, Front bel Fulton
Hart James, col wat, Bevan's Court
Hatton Hugh, overseer, Edgmont bel Free
Hatfield James, machinist, Liberty ab Potter
Haverstick John, cordw, James bel Concord
Haviland Rev. Arthur, Edgmont bel Larkin
Hawes James, cordw, Uplind below Liberty
Haycock Jacob & Co., machinists, Filbert ab Front
Haycock Jacob, machinist, Broad bel Upland
Healy George C., oyster saloon, James bel Market
Heathcote John, cord, Front bel Fulton
Heathcote Andrew, operat, Front bel Fulton
Heffron John, coachman, at Dr. Young's, James bel Fulton
Henderson Charles S., moulder, Filbert ab Edgmont
Henderson George, cordw, Market bel R R
Helms Isaac, lab, back of Second bel Essex
Hetzell Wm., clerk, Clinton ab Welsh
Hibberd John, att'y, Penn Buildings, Market
Hibberd Ellen, wid, Quarry bel Liberty

Hibberd Henry, lab, Quarry bel Liberty
Hibberd Daniel, operat, do do do
Hickman J. L., carpt, Free ab Welsh
Higgins James, carter, Work bel Market
Hill Howard, capt, Filbert bel Market
Hinkson & Baker, coal & lumber, Edgmont bel R R
Hinkson Fred. J., tanner, Edgmont ab James
Hinkson H. M., gent, Edgmont bel James
Hinkson Orpha, gentw, Edgmont bel James
Hinkson & Slawter, house painters, Work ab Market
Hinkson Joseph, gent, Clinton bel Crosby
Hinkson W., lumber merch, Welsh ab R R
Hinkson John, carpt, Larkin ab Upland
Hinkson & Bell, tannery, Edgmont ab James
Hirosson Wm., operat, Quarry bel Liberty
Holt Sarah, wid, Edgmont & Work
Holt Joseph, machinist, Larkin ab Edgmont
Holt Joseph, druggist, Broad ab Mechanic
Holt Amos, tailor, Broad ab Mechanic
Holt James, operat, Madison bel Liberty
Holt Elizabeth, gentw, James & Concord
Holmes Edward, operat, North ab R R
Hollin Nancy, wid, Upland bel Cochran
Honnor John, wat, Broad ab Upland
Hood Rachel, col laundress, Free bel R R
Hood Rev. George, Chester Fem. Seminary, Broad ab Upland
Horrocks Francis, operat, Liberty bel Upland
Howes E. S., grocery, Market bel R R
Howarth James, weaver, R R ab Welsh
Howarth John, operat, Front bel Fulton
Howarth Joseph, operat, Second bel do
Hubbell R. H., Gas Works, Free bel Upland
Hughes Patrick, machinist, Madison bel Liberty
Hull James, col lab, Powell's Court
Huley B., col lab, Concord opp Fifth
Hunter George, lab, Larkin ab Edgmont

Hunter Wm., brush maker, Logan ab Edgmont
Hunter Wm., cordw, Edgmont ab Logan
Hunter Joseph, wheelwright, Broad & Upland
Huston Esther, wid, Free ab Upland
Huston Saml, Quarryman, Darby R bel Ridley creek

I & J

Irving Thomas, paper maker, Welsh ab R R
Irving & Leiper. Barndennock mills, Front ab Franklin
Ivins Francis, machinist, Upland bel Market
Jackson James, operat, Free bel R R
Jackson Wm., lab, Free ab Edgmont
Jackson Washington, operat, Quarry bel Liberty
Jester Wm. F., h paint & pap hang Edgmont ab James
Jefferson Rev. Benj., col lab, Welsh bel James
Johnston John, lab, Concord ab Fifth
Johnston Samuel, col lab, James ab Fulton
Johnston John, machinist, Market bel Filbert
Johnson Samuel, Bevan's Court
Johnson John, col lab, Welsh ab Filbert
Johnstone Ebenezer, mason, Deshong ab Edgmont
Johnstone George, do do do do
Jones Samuel, col lab, Welsh ab Filbert
Jones Perry, col lab, Welsh bel James
Jones George, col porter, Market near Powell's Court
Jones Jona., col fence mkr, Welsh bel James
Jones Mary, operat, Fifth ab Concord

K

Kane Wm., cordw, Edgmont bel Liberty
Kay Edward, operat, Upland ab Broad
Kelley Wm., cordw, James ab Welsh
Kelley Esther, wid, Work ab Edgmont
Kelley P. P., mail carrier, Work ab Edgmont
Kelley Esther R., milliner, do do do
Kelley Mary, wid, Front bel Fulton
Kelley Owen, lab, Darby R ab Cochran
Kelley Patrick, quarryman, Darby R bel Ridley creek

Kenworthy J. W., coal merchant, Broad & Darby R
Kenworthy Charles, clerk, Larkin bel Mechanic
Kerlin Wm., wat, Work bel Welsh
Kerlin A. L., wid, Edgmont ab R R
Kerlin Martha, wid, James ab Penn
Kesterd Bridget, gentw, Broad ab Mechanic
Kinney Mary, wid, Edgmont bel Liberty
King Rachel, wid, Logan ab Madison
Kirk Mary, wid, Front bel Fulton
Kirk Ellen, operat, Front bel Fulton
Knipe John, lab, Logan bel Quarry
Knott Wm., machinist, Welsh ab Work
Knowles James, cotton mills, Front bel Essex
Knott James, machinist, Welsh ab Work
Koehler Michael, clothier, Penn Buildings
Krauch Christian, lager beer saloon, Edgmont & Larkin
Kutzhler Jer., operat, back of Free bel Market

L

Ladomus Jos., watches & jewellery, Market bel Work
Ladue J. W., machinist, Potter bel Liberty
Lamey Wm., cordw, R R ab Upland
Lamplugh S. R., house painter, Work ab Market
Lambson Wm., carpt, Penn & Front
Lane Park, cordw, Welsh ab R R
Lane Hannah, wid, Free bel Upland
Lane Joel, clerk, do do do
Lane Thomas, blacksmith, Second bel Fulton
Laney Michael, lab, Edgmont & Liberty
Lancaster Sarah, col wid, Welsh ab Filbert
Larkin J. M., druggist, Market & James
Larkin C. C. & A., steam planing mill, sash factory, Broad & Potter
Larkin Nathan, sash maker, &c., Broad bel Upland
Larkin John, Jr., gent, Broad ab Madison
Larkin Lewis, merchant, Broad & Upland
Larkin Charles C., sash mkr, &c., Larkin bel Madion

Latch George, operat, Work ab Edgmont
Latch Lusan, wid, Work bel Market
Lear Charles, drover, Free ab Market
Lear Sophia, gentw, Free ab Market
Lear Wm., boots & shoes, Market ab James
Leary James, operat, Larkin ab Edgmont
Lebo John, lab, Darby R ab Larkin
Leckey Robert, select boarding school, Second bel Franklin
Lee Edward, operat, Mechanic bel Liberty
Lee John, operat, Potter ab Broad
Lees Daniel, operat, Upland ab Logan
Lees James, machinist, Broad ab Mechanic
Leiper Thomas J., manuf, James bel Market
Lenney James, cordw, Market bel R R
Leonard Mary, wid, Front bel Parker
Lester John, operat, broad bel Mechanic
Lester James, victualler, Larkin ab Upland
Lever Edward, operat, Fifth ab Concord
Lewis Edward, pattern maker, Edgmont bel Free
Lewis Jerry, lab, Powell's Court
Linton Matt., lab, Filbert bel Welsh
Lindsay Henry H., gent, Filbert bel Market
Lisle Rebecca, wid, Front bel Penn
Little Thomas, tanner, Filbert bel Welsh
Liversidge Thos., dry goods & groc, Edgmont & Broad
Loatman Martha, col, Welsh bel James
Logan John, lab, Providence R ab Upland
Lombaert H. J., auditor Penna R R Co, Second ab Franklin
Long Samuel, Jr., pattern mkr, James ab Welsh
Long John, carpt, Free bel Market
Long Joshua, do do do do
Long Thomas R., carpt, Mechanic bel Liberty
Long Teresa, tailoress, Penn ab Second
Longbothom John, victualler, Franklin ab James
Longbothom John, meat shop, James bel Market

Lowe Wm., cordw, Upland bel Liberty
Lukens W. B. carpt, Potter bel Liberty
Lyons Crossman, gent, Free & Welsh
Lyons Rose W., wid, Filbert ab Market
Lytle Andrew, farmer, Concord ab R R
Lytle Samuel, do do do

M

Mackey Robt, lab, Upland a Liberty
Macartney Robt, operat, Work bel Market
Madgin Thos, farmer, James bel Fulton
Magraw Martin, carpt, Fulton bel Second
Malany Jas, cord, James ab Welsh
Malony Hannah, groc, a provisions, Market bel Free
Malin Wm, carpt, North ab R R
Mann Michael, cord, Front bel Parker
Manuel Jas, operat, Filbert ab Market
Marshall Margt, operat, Franklin bel Second
Marshall John, operat, Mechanic bel Liberty
Martine J L, cord, James bel Essex
Martine Abm., saddler, James ab Essex
Marshall Wm, operat, Franklin bel Second
Marshman Chandler, cord James bel Market
Marlor Eliz, wid, Work bel Welsh
Marlor Wm., operat, Work bel Welsh
Marlor Joseph, operat, Work bel Welsh
Martin Adeline, tin ware, Market ab James
Mason Thomas, teamster, Front ab Filbert
Matson Asa, engineer, Penn & Front
M'Arthur Archibald, ship carpt, Market ab Filbert
M'Arann Wm. A., cordw, James ab Penn
M'Call Wm., cattle dealer, Clinton bel Crosby
M'Call Robert, tobacconist, Market ab Work
M'Clare Hugh, lab, back of Second bel Essex
M'Collum Susan, dry goods & gro Market bel R R
M'Connell Mr., cordw, Market bel R R
M'Connell Robert, cordw, James bel Penn
M'Collin J. G., cash. bank Del. Co., Market & James

M'Catherty Edward, clerk, Free & Welsh
M'Cluskey Henry, coach painter, Free ab Welsh
M'Clymont James, pattern maker, Welsh bel R R
M'Clay James, lab, Fulton bel James
M'Clymont John, machinist, W elsh bel R R
M'Cullough Michael, cab mkr, Work ab Edgmont
M'Collum Francis, wat, Broad ab Potter
M'Cormick James, machinist, Broad ab Mechanic
M'Cullough John, lab, North ab R R
M'Cabe Francis, machinist, Second bel Fulton
M'Cann Wm. A., coal yard, James ab Penn
M'Cann Wm. A., boot & shoe store, James bel Market
M'Devitt Wm., stone cutter, Market bel R R
M'Fadgen James, lab, Darby R ab Cochran
M'Gonegal Patrick, quarryman, Darby R bel Liberty
M'Grath Henry, grocery, Filbert ab Market
M'Ginty Hugh, lab, Liberty ab Madison
M'Ginly Michael, lab, Cochran bel Darby R
M'Gorlick Mrs. W., wid, Market ab Filbert
M'Ilvain Spencer, farmer, Darby R near Ridley creek
M'Ilvain Henry, do do do do
M'Kinzie John, tailor, Penn bel James
M'Kinney David, quarryman, Darby R near Ridley cr
M'Kinley Dennis, quarryman, do do do
M'Kinzey John, tailor, Penn ab Second
M'Keever John B., mercht, Welsh bel Edgmont
M'Kenney Patrick, quarryman, Darby R ab Liberty
M'Kinley Catharine, operat, do do do
M'Kinney James, lab do do R R
M'Keever Nancy, wid, Edgmont ab Broad
M'Kendrick Catharine, operat, Front bel Fulton
M'Kendrick Sarah, do do do
M'Kendrick Annie, do do do
M'Laughlin Daniel, lab, Edgmont ab Welsh
M'Laughlin Ellen, wid, Edgmont ab Filbert
M'Laren Hannah, confec, Market & Filbert
M'Laughlin John, lab, Free & Welsh
M'Leary John, lab, Mechanic bel Liberty

M'Lay Wm., cordw, Broad bel Upland
M'Laughlin Andrew, lab, Liberty bel Upland
M'Laughlin John, stone cutter, Darby R ab R R
M'Lean John, operat, Fifth ab Concord
M'Mahan Mary, wid, Providence R ab Upland
M'Miniman Daniel, lab, do do do
M'Neal Arch., cordw, Filbert ab Edgmont
M'Nall Mr., bricklayer, Edgmont ab Filbert
M'Miniman Edward, lab, Providence R ab Upland
Mendon James, machinist, Madison bel Liberty
Mendon Wm., operat, do do do
Merritt George, blacksmith, Front bel Essex
Middleton Eliz., operat, Edgmont bel R R
Mills George, cordw, Edgmont bel Filbert
Mills Samuel, cordw, Market ab Filbert
Mills Wm., operat, Darby R ab Broad
Mills James, lab, Second bel Fulton
Mills Wm., saddler, James bel Penn
Mills Jacob, gent, do do do
Millins George, operat, Madison ab Broad
Miller Lewis, machinist, Broad ab Upland
Miller Maria, col wid, Bevan's Court
Miller Lewis, machinist, Broad & Darby R
Miller Richard, merch tailor, Market bel R R
Millington Ellen, wid, Work bel Welsh
Milley Wm., operat, James bel Essex
Milley John, operat, do ab Franklin
Milns George, operat, Madison bet Broad & Liberty
Minshall Wm. A., cabinet mkr & undertaker, Free ab Market
Minshall E. R., groc & prov, Market & Work
Mirkil Thomas, agent, Market ab Filbert
Mirkil Isaiah, collector, do do do
Mitchell John A., hats, leather, shoe findings, James bel Market
Mitchell Manuel col lab, Bevan's Court
Molyneaux John, oyster saloon Market bel James
Monroe Wm. H., dentist, Market ab Work

Montgomery Samuel carpt, Front bel Essex
Montgomery John, carpt, Second bel Fulton
Montgomery Alex., operat, do do do
Moore Thomas, gun & locksmith, James bel Market
Morris George, moulder, Market bel R R
Morris J. H., machinist, Second bel Fulton
Morris John, wat, Front ab Essex
Morris Mgt., wid, Front bel Fulton
Morrison James, lab, Free ab Upland
Morrison D. W., carpt, Penn bel James
Morgan James, operat, Upland bel Liberty
Morgan James, operat. Larkin ab Upland
Morton Dr. Charles K., Edgmont near Providence R
Morton Justis, printer, Market & Powell's Court
Moulder James, ship carpt, Front bel Fulton
Mousely Wm., plasterer, Providence R bel Potter
Murray Charles, col lab, Filbert & Welsh
Murray Wm., cordw, Market bel R R
Murray Abm., lab, Concord ab Fifth
Murphey Wm., col lab, Free ab Edgmont
Murphey Nickolas, lab, Filbert bel Welsh
Marshall Ann, operat, Franklin bel Second

N

Neal John, lab, Welsh bel James
News John brickmaker, Liberty bel Upland
News Wm, brickmaker, Franklin ab James
Newell Robt, dyer, Front bel Fulton
Newell Joseph, engineer, Front bel Fulton
Nelson Jas D, wharf builder, James ab Welsh
Noblit Anna, wid, Edgmont bel R R
Noblit Dell, ship carpt, Edgmont bel R R
Noblit Thos, operat, Free ab Market
Noden Thos, operat, Front bel Fulton
Noden Jona, operat, Front bel Fulton
Nuttall Thos, gent, Quarry ab Broad
Nuttall Levi, grocery, Welsh bel Edgmont
Nugent Annie, col, wid, Filbert bel Welsh

Nugent Leah, col, wid, Bevan's Court

O

Oat Israel, cord, Concord ab Fifth
O'Donaldson Wm, lab, Logan ab Quarry
O'Donnall Patrick, lab, Second ab Fulton
Ogleby Robt, operat, Broad ab Mechanic
O'Hara Jas, lab, Broad bel Darby R
Omensetter J H, teacher, Penn ab Front
O'Neil John, carpt, Front bel Fulton
O'Rourke Timothy, mason, Darby R bel Cochran
O'Rourke Wm, mason, Filbert bel Market
Oreal Thos J, carpt, Work ab Edgmont
Orey Jas, operat, Liberty bel Darby R
Ott Henry, tallow chandler, Edgmont ab James
Ott Maurice, do do do do do
Ottey Wesley, blacksmith, Larkin & Upland
Ottey Redmon, carpt, North bel Cochran
Owen Dr. Joshua, Edgmont opp Work
Owens Wm., wat, North bel Cochran

P

Paist Jesse W., carpt, Market ab Filbert
Palmer Samuel, brick mkr, Franklin ab James
Palmer James, coach trimmer, Free & Welsh
Patterson Alex., machinist, Broad ab Mechanic
Pattison Wm., cordw, James bel Franklin
Pennell Edmund, farmer, James bel Fulton
Pennell J. L., victualler, James bel Fulton
Pennell S. J., wid, James ab Welsh
Pennell J. & C. D., lumber & coal, Edgmont ab James
Pennell Jona., lumber merch, do do do
Pennell C. D., do do do do do
Pendergast John, grocery, James ab Edgmont
Perkins Abm. R., farmer, do bel Fulton
Peterson Joseph, col wat, Welsh bel James
Picup Mary, Upland bel Larkin
Pickels James C., china & glass ware, Market ab James

Philips Catharine, wid, Front bel Fulton
Philips John, wat, Filbert bel Market
Platt James, blacksmith, James & Fulton
Plummer E. H., cordw, Upland bel Liberty
Porter Wm., quarryman, Darby R ab Liberty
Porter James, lab, R R ab Upland
Porter Charles, wat, Darby R ab Liberty
Porter Jenkins, col lab, James ab Fulton
Potter Rev. Alonzo, Potter ab Morton
Porter Dr. James J., Welsh & Delaware river
Potts George W., col porter, Welsh bel James
Pike Rachel, wid, Work ab Market
Pike Isaiah, carpt, Filbert bel Market
Pike Isaac, engineer, do do do
Pike Benj., wat, Edgmont ab Filbert
Pratt H. D., harness mkr, James ab Penn
Pratt H. D., saddler, Free ab Market
Preston Samuel, lab, Filbert bel Welsh
Preston Dr. C., James bel Penn
Preston Henry C., col lab, Welsh ab Filbert
Price J. Wade, books & stationery, James bel Market
Price Samuel A., gent, do do do
Price John C., brickmkr, do do do
Price Wm. G., do Filbert bel Market
Price J. C. & W. G., brick yard, Liberty & Potter
Price D. T., house painter, Madison ab Liberty
Price Elizabeth, wid, James bel Concord
Priegel J. G., house painter, Madison bel Liberty
Priestly Samuel, operat, Front bel Fulton
Pryor Warner, col lab, Welsh ab Filbert
Pullen Samuel, wat, Filbert ab Market
Purnsley Rachel, wid, Welsh bel James
Pusey Lydia, gentw, Edgmont opp Free
Pyvell Sarah A., wid, Edgmont ab Welsh
Pyvell Wm., agent, Upland bel Larkin

Q

Quinn Abrm., carpt., Edgmont bel Free

R

Rambo Wm., lab, Market & Filbert
Raney Joseph, plasterer, Front bel Penn
Rappernecker Wm., cord, Liberty ab Upland
Rathburn C. W., gent, Welsh bel R R
Rathburn Mrs. Rebecca, private school, Welsh bel R R
Rawcliffe James, variety store, Free & Edgmont
Reddin Absalom, col lab, Welsh ab Filbert
Reed Bradford, lab, Work bel Welsh
Reeves Prudence, col wid, Bevan's court
Rees Isaac, engineer, Broad & Mechanic
Rex Dr. Geo., Second bel Parker
Richards Deborah, wid, Welsh ab Work
Riddle Sallie, teacher, Welsh bel R R
Riddle James, teacher, Welsh bel R R
Riddle Geo. S., wheelright, Welsh bel R R
Ritchie Samuel, operat, Fulton bel James
Riter Jacob, ship carpt, Edgmont bel Free
Rhoads Joseph, col carter, Powell's court
Rhodes Joseph, trader, Madison & Liberty
Rhoads Wm., bricklayer, Filbert ab Market
Roach E. W. & T. E., commercial academy, Edgmont & Welsh
Roberts Howard, livery stable, Free ab Welsh
Roan Geo., lab, Cochran bel Darby R
Roberts Wm., agent, Free ab Welsh
Roberts Mary, gentw, Free bel Market
Robinson John, Essex bel Second
Roach E. W., teacher, Edgmont & Welsh
Robinson John S., machinist, Essex bel Second
Roach T. E., teacher, Edgmont & Welsh
Roach Thomas, ambrotypist, Edgmont & Welsh
Rodeback Allen, machinist, James ab Franklin
Rose Samuel J., brickmaker, Upland & Liberty
Rosevelt Jas. E. R., livery stable, Work bel Market
Rosevelt James, livery stable, James ab Market

Rosevelt J. G., Market bel R R
Rosevelt Theo. V., tobacconist, Market bel R R
Ross Richard, carpt, Essex bel Second
Ross Thomas, carpt, James bel Essex
Ross Richard, capt, Penn & Front
Ross Francis, lab, Upland bel Liberty
Ross Patrick, carter, Upland bel Liberty
Ross John, lab, Providence R ab Upland
Ross John, house painter, Edgmont ab Welsh
Ross Hamilton, col wat, Welsh ab Filbert
Rothwell Isaac, col lab, Bevan's court
Roxburgh S. A., operat, Work ab Market
Rulan Job, gent, Edgmont ab James
Rumford Washington, bricklayer, James ab Franklin
Rumford Absalom, col lab, Bevan's court
Rumford Wm., col wat, Welsh ab Filbert
Rump Edward, col lab, Bevan's court
Russell John, blacksmith, Welsh ab R R
Russell Jeremiah, wat, Market ab Filbert
Rutter Blythe, wheelwright, Market ab James
Rutter Esther A., milliner, Market ab James
Rutter John, col lab, Free bel R R
Ruth Rev. John, Clinton bel Crosby

S

Sample Robert, operat, Franklin bel Second
Sample Ann, wid, Edgmont ab Providence R
Saunders J., lab, Bevan's court
Schofield Edward, operat, Edgmont ab Logan
Schofield Wm., grocery, Broad & Mechanic
Schofield James, operat, Front bel Fulton
Scureman Wm., stoves & tinner, Market ab James
Scureman John, moulder, Free ab Welsh
Scott Francis, operat, Larkin ab Edgmont
Scott John, engineer, Free ab Market
Scott John, teamster, Fulton bel Second
Seal Wm. A., plasterer, James ab Penn
Seary James, carpt, Free ab Welsh

Seyfort John, livery, Work bel Market
Sharpless J. M., packet & lime wharf, Market & Del river
Sharpless Wm., merch, James & Franklin
Starrett F. J., print, Market & Powell's court
Stain Emily, dress maker, Free bel Upland
Shaw Samuel, gent., James ab Concord
Shaw Arnold, operat, Broad & Potter
Shepherd Geo., foundryman, Work bel Welsh
Shepherd Wm., watchman, Second bel Fulton
Shepherdson Wm., carpt, Second bel Fulton
Shipps David, groceries & feed, Market & Work
Shoemaker Fred., cord, Mechanic ab Broad
Shroder Chas., tinman, Market ab Filbert
Simpson James, tailor, Penn ab Second
Simpson James, tailor, James bel Market
Simpson Mgt., gentw, Penn bel James
Sines Mary, wid, Welsh & Clinton
Sinex John A., trader, Fifth ab Concord
Sinex Jacob, ship builder, Front bel Franklin
Singleton Wm., weaver, Welsh bel Edgmont
Singles Wm., currier, Front bel Filbert
Slaughter Lewis, house painter, Broad bel Upland
Smedley Geo. L., clerk, Edgmont bel James
Smedley Ellis, dry goods, groceries, hardware, Market Square
Smith John, victualler, Liberty bel Darby R
Smith John, operat, Second bel Fulton
Smith Francis, gent, Liberty bel Darby R
Smith Robert, operat, Free bel Upland
Smith Wm., col brickmaker, Edgmont ab Work
Smith Mary, store, Edgmont bel James
Smith Geo., operat, Free bel Upland
Smith Martha, wid, Free & Welsh
Smith Joseph, tailor, Broad & Upland
Smith Samuel R., R R House, Market & R R
Smith Joseph, carpt, Second ab Fulton
Sneath G. H., carpt, Welsh bel R R

Snelgrove Geo., baker, Broad & Upland
Spalacy John, lab, Second bel Parker
Spane Michael, cord, Work bel Market
Stacy D. B., merch, Market bel Work
Starr Samuel, coal & wood, James ab Penn
Steel John, bricklayer, Cochran & North
Stephens James, manuf cottons, Market & Work
Stevenson Jeremiah, victualler, James bel Essex
Stephenson Samuel, ship builder, Penn bel James
Stewart John, cord, Filbert ab Market
Stewart Joseph, col lab, Welsh ab Filbert
Stewart Eliz., operat, Madison bel Liberty
St Leger Daniel, machinist, Liberty bel Potter
Stewart Jacob, cord, Edgmont ab Providence R
Sproull Rev. A. W., Clinton ab Welsh
Sproull Eliz., wid, Fulton bel Second
Story Chas. A., tobacconist, Deshong ab Edgmont
Stokes Henrietta, dress maker, Edgmont ab Broad
Stokely Samuel, ship carpt, Free ab Edgmont
Struthers Alex., operat, Franklin ab Front
Strickland Amos A., house painter, Work ab Edgmont
Sullivan Wm., kerosene oil store, James bel Market
Sullivan Sarah, gentw. Free ab Market
Sullivan John, ship carpt, Free ab Market
Sweeny Wm., box maker, Larkin ab Edgmont
Sykes Wm., operat, James bel Fulton
Story Chas. A., tobacconist, Deshong ab Edgmont
Stokes Henrietta, dress maker, Edgmont ab Broad

T

Talley James, plasterer, Front bel Penn
Taylor Sarah S., operat, cor James & Franklin
Taylor Wm. J., operat, do do do
Taylor Samuel, gent, do do do
Taylor Alfred, teacher, Second ab Franklin
Taylor Henry B., clerk, do do do
Taylor Samuel E., engineer, James bel Essex

Taylor Wm., clerk, Penn bel Second
Taylor Wm., cordw, Edgmont ab Providence R
Taylor Lewis, brickmkr, Upland bel Liberty
Taylor Charles, gent, Larkin bel Mechanic
Taylor Robert S., machinist, Welsh ab R R
Taylor Richard, gent's furnishing store, Market bel RR
Taylor Capt R. S., wat, James ab Welsh
Taylor Lewis P., bricklayer, do do do
Taylor Capt. Luther M., wat, do do do
Taylor Enos, clerk, Market bel R R
Taylor Joseph, coach mkr, cor Free & Welsh
Taylor W. H. M., do do do do do
Taylor Edwd, blacksmith, do do do do
Taylor Jona., machinist, Broad ab Mechanic
Taylor Joseph, agent, railroad station
Taylor Joseph, operat, cor Broad & Upland
Temple John A., freight agent, cor Edgmont & R R
Tingler Lewis, baker, cor Broad & Upland
Tippin Leonard, operat, James ab Franklin
Thatcher Lewis & Wm., sash & door factory, Front & Crosby
Thatcher Lewis, sash mkr, James ab Penn
Thomas John col ostler, Free ab Welsh
Thomas Margaret D., teacher, cor Welsh & Work
Thornly John, oil manuf, Second bel Parker
Thomson D. B., house painter, cor Broad & Edgmont
Thomson George, operat, Front bel Fulton
Todd Jona., operat, Broad bel Madison
Troth Jacob, bricklayer, James ab Welsh
Train James, cordw, James bel Franklin
Tranks Benj., col cordw, cor Market & Powell's Court
Trout Wm., pat mkr, Work bel Market
Trout Wm. H., do do do do
Turner Samuel, operat, Broad bel Madison
Turner Richard, operat, Edgmont ab Logan
Turner James, engineer, do do Liberty
Turner Stephen, col lab, Powell's Court
Turner Wm., salesman, cor Edgmont & Broad

Turner George, operat, Upland bel Liberty

U

Ulrich Samuel, Justice of Peace, James ab Penn
Ulrich John, agent, do bel Essex

V

Valentine T. J., green grocery, James ab Penn
Valentine Theo., col barber, cor James & Market Square
Vanhorn Wm., operat, Liberty bel Madison
Vanhartsdale Joseph, clerk, do do do
Vandegrift Sarah, wid, Market ab Filbert
Vanhorn Nathan, operat, Liberty bel Potter
Vanzant Jane E., milliner, Penn bel James
Vanzant N., operat, Front bel Fulton
Vanzant Adeline, operat, do do do
Vanzant Esther J., do do do do
Vanzant Theo. A., do do do do
Vernon Samuel, carpt, Broad bel Upland
Vernon J. B., carpt, Front ab Essex

W

Wagner Jacob, sawyer, Front ab Essex
Walter Y. S., Ed Del Co Rep, cor Market & James
Warren Samuel, furniture store, Penn bel James
Warner Wm., gent, Edgmont ab Liberty
Warner Penrose, miller, Edgmont ab Liberty
Warren John, operat, Larkin ab Edgmont
Wantine Wm., wat, Cochran bel Darby R
Waters Sarah, wid, Potter bel Liberty
Watson Jane, col wid, Darby R ab Larkin
Watson Benj., col wat, Welsh ab Filbert
Waters James, col brickmaker, Potter ab Liberty
Wallace Henry, col lab, Bevan's court
Wallace Archibald, jr., operat, back of Free bel Market
Wallace " " " "
West Keziah, gentw, Free bel Welsh
Weaver Isaac, flour and feed store

Welsh John, carpt, Work ab Edgmont
Weidner Chas. A. & Co., Chester Iron Found, Edgmont bel R R
Weidner Chas. A., Welsh ab R R
Wellington Mary, operat, Broad ab Mechanic
Webb James, dry goods, Broad bel Mechanic
West Eli, roller coverer, Liberty bel Darby R
Welser Benj. B., cordw, cor Upland & Liberty
Weaver Joseph, carpt, James ab Fulton
Weaver Jane, operat, James ab Fulton
West Spencer, col teamster, Bevan's court
Weaver Geo. W., postmaster, James bel Market
Weaton Mary, wid, Front ab Filbert
Wheaton Joseph, lab, Filbert bel Welsh
Wheaton Andw., engineer, " "
White Benj., col lab., Free ab Upland
White Nathan, col teacher, Filbert ab Market
White Cath., col wid, Liberty ab Edgmont
Whiting Geo., produce, cor Clinton & Welsh
Whitehead Geo., weaver, cor Filbert & Welsh
Whitaker Margt., wid, Madison bel Liberty
Wilson David, col confect, Market bel James
Wilson Joseph, clerk, Market ab Filbert
Wilson Ann, col, Edgmont bel R R
Wilson Geo., National Hotel, cor Edgmont & James
Wilson Wm., gent., cor Edgmont & James
Wilson Robert, operat, Work bel Welsh
Wilson James, lab, Liberty bel Quarry
Wilson Jonathan, wat, " " "
Wilson George, carpt, Mechanic bel Liberty
Wilson Charles, brickmkr, " "
Wilson Jacob, brkmak, Liberty ab Mechanic
Williams Samuel, lab, James bel Fulton
Williams John, cordw, James bel Essex
Williams Anna B., wid, Upland bel Larkin
Williams Benjamin, carpt, Edgmont ab Providence R
Williams Francis, operat, Welsh ab James
Williams Chas., tailor, James bel Market

Williams Ellenora B., saleswoman, James bel Market
Williams John, bricklayer, Essex bel Second
Williamson John, operat, Quarry bel Liberty
Williamson Abigail, gentw, James bel Franklin
Wild John, dry goods & grocs, Market bel James
Wild Eliz., milliner, cor Edgmont & Liberty
Willey William, operat, Franklin ab Front
Willey Wm. K., " " " "
Willey Jesse K., " " " "
Willey Margt. K., " " " "
Witton John, tailor, Second bel Fulton
Wilkey James, pat maker, Filbert ab Market
Winslow Mary, wid, Welsh ab R R
Wilkinson James, operat, Upland bel Liberty
Wiley James, operat, Mechanic ab Broad
Wood John, meat store, Market bel James
Wood Margt., laundress, Fulton bel James
Wood Thomas, operat, Fourth ab Concord
Wood John, col wat, Bevan's court
Wolf Martin, lab, Powell's court
Wollcot John, grocery, Upland bel Liberty
Woodhead Alfred, operat, cor James & Franklin
Worthington Mr., carter, Providence R ab Upland
Worthington Nat., lab, " " "
Wright Alex., clerk, Broad bel Madison
Wright Harrison, operat, Deshong ab Edgmont
Wright Lucy, wid, Upland bel Larkin
Wright James, machinist, North bel Cochran
Wunderlich Geo., meat & prov, cor Market & Free

Y

Young Dr. Wm., James bel Fulton
Young Dr. Edward, James ab Welsh
Younker Margt., wid, Edgmont bel Free
Younker James, boil mak, " " "
Younker Bennager, mach, " " "

STATISTICS.

CHURCHES.

FRIENDS.—Meeting House on Market street, between James and Graham.

EPISCOPAL.—Church on James street, between Market and Welsh. The Pastor, Rev. James Kendig, having resigned, in consequence the pulpit is supplied *pro tempore* by Rev. Mr. Talbot. Number of communicants, 120. Children in Sabbath School, 150. Time of regular Sabbath service in Winter, 10½ o'clock, A. M., and 7 P. M.; in Summer, 10 A. M., and 7½ P. M. Prayer meeting every Wednesday evening. Superintendent of Sabbath School, Dr. J. M. Allen.

Wardens.—Senior Warden, John Larkin, Jr.; Junior Warden, Dr. J. M. Allen.

Vestrymen—John Larkin, Jr., Dr. J. M. Allen, Charles C. Larkin, J. B. M'Keever, J. G. Johnson, James Cochran, D. B. Thompson, Crossman Lyons, James Campbell.

METHODIST.—Church on Free street, west of Market. Pastor, Rev. John Ruth. Regular services are held every Sabbath at 10½ o'clock, A. M., and 7 P. M.

Trustees—David Abbot, Daniel Birtwell, Edward Congleton, Thomas Liversidge, John Hall, Jacob Sinex, John Sinex, Wm. Sharpless, Joseph Taylor.

Stewards.—David Abbot, John Thompson, Thos. Liversidge, William Sharpless, Daniel Birtwell, John Sinex, Jacob Sinex, John Hall.

Superintendent of Sunday School.—Wm. Flavill.

Catholic.—Church on Edgmont street, south of Larkin. Pastor, Rev. A. Haviland. Congregation, 1500. Regular Sabbath service at 7½ and 10½ o'clock, A. M., and Vespers at 3½ P. M. Number of children in Sunday School, 200; teachers, 16; hours of attendance from 8 to 10 A. M. and 2 to 3 P. M. Superintendent, Rev. A. Haviland.

Presbyterian.—Church corner of Clinton and Welsh streets. Pastor, Rev. A. W. Sproull. Communicants, 110. Children in Sabbath School, 200, having 16 teachers. Regular Sabbath service in Winter at 10½ o'clock, A. M., and 7 P. M. In Summer, 10 A. M. and 7½ P. M. Lecture every Wednesday evening at 7½ o'clock. Prayer meeting every Friday evening.

Elders—Jno. Cochran, James Ridley, Joseph Hinkson, Jno. Hard.

PUBLIC SCHOOLS.

High or Grammar School.—Franklin, north of James street. No. 1, Boys, taught by Mr. J. H. Omensetter. No. 2, Girls, taught by Miss Thomas. Branches taught, spelling, reading, writing, arithmetic, algebra, mensuration, geography, grammar, history and composition.

Secondary Department.—No. 1, boys, taught by J. Riddle, corner of Free and Welsh. No. 2, girls, taught by Miss A. E. Wright, corner of Free and Welsh. No. 3, boys and girls, taught by Miss Sallie Riddle, Franklin, north of James. No. 4, boys, taught by Mr. J. B. Donaldson, corner of Logan and Madison. Branches taught, spelling, reading, writing, arithmetic and geography.

Primary Department.—No. 1, boys and girls, taught by Miss C. Boner, corner of Free and Welsh.

No. 2, boys and girls, taught by Mrs. Harris, Franklin north of James. No. 3, boys and girls, taught by Miss Greig, principal, and Miss Ulrich, assistant, corner of Logan and Madison. Branches taught, alphabet, spelling and reading.

COLORED SCHOOL.—Boys and girls, taught by Nathan S. White, Filbert, east of Market.

Number of pupils:—

Grammar school,		boys,	35
"	"	girls,	57
Secondary dep.,		boys,	137
"	"	girls,	87
Primary	"	boys,	133
"	"	girls,	137
Colored	"	boys,	30
"	"	girls,	25
Whole number of pupils,			641

School term, 10 months.

Average salary of male teachers per month,	$36 25
" " " female " " "	27 14
Amount of teacher's salaries per annum	3350 00
" " expenditure for books,	275 00
" " tax levied in 1859,	5194 00
Real estate of department valued at	12000 00

SCHOOL DIRECTORS.—Fred. J. Hinkson, Stephen Cloud, Alex. W. Wright, Dr. John S. Morton, Samuel Shaw, Wm. Hinkson. Regular meetings of the Board are held upon the first Wednesday of each month.

SCHOOLS.—Public, Franklin north of James; corner of Free and Welsh; and corner of Logan and Madison.

Private.—Chester Female Seminary, by Rev. Geo. Hood, Broad street, above Upland. Select Boarding School, by Robert Leckey, Second street below Franklin.

BOROUGH OFFICERS.

Chief Burgess—Robert Gartside.
Treasurer—John Brooks.
Town Clerk—James Riddle.
Town Council—James Campbell, Joseph Ladomus, James Bell, John Larkin, Jr., Abm. Blakely, Dr. Wm. Young, Benj. Gartside, Wm. Lear, Robert R. Dutton.
Auditor—Job Rulon.
Judge—Joseph Taylor.
Inspector—Amos Gartside.
Assessor—Isaiah H. Mirkle.
Constable—Charles Williams.
Lamp Lighters—Francis Williams, M. Faraday, Jesse Gallagher.

Council meets upon the first Monday of every month. Tax levied for Borough purposes for 1859, $3594 64. Borough debt, $13,000.

POST OFFICE.

James street, below Market. Office hours from 7 o'clock, A. M. until 7 o'clock, P. M.; on Sundays from 12 M. until 1 o'clock. Arrivals and departures of the mails:

Northern mail arrives at 9 o'clock, A. M. and 11.30 P.M.
Southern " " " 2 " P. M.
Ridleyville and Leiperville arrives at 1 o'clock, P. M.
Northern mail departs at 1.30 P. M., and 8.30 P. M.
Southern " " " 8.30, A. M.
Ridleyville and Leiperville departs at 9 oclock, A. M.
Postmaster—Geo. W. Weaver.

BANK OF DELAWARE COUNTY.

The Bank of Delaware County, was chartered 21st

of March, 1814. It is located at the southwest corner of James and Market streets.

John Newbold was the first President,
Dr. Jonas Preston, second President,
Pierce Crosby, third President,
John Kerlin, fourth President,
Jesse J. Maris, fifth President.
Preston Eyre, was the first Cashier,
Charles S. Folwell, second Cashier,
F. I. Hinkson, third Cashier,
James G. McCollin, fourth Cashier.'

Capital paid in, $200,000. Discount days, Mondays and Thursdays, at 10 o'clock A. M. Closed on the fourth of July and Christmas.

LINES OF TRAVEL.

Philaldelphia and Wilmington Steamboats leave Chester as follows:

SUMMER.

For Philadelphia, 7.30 A. M., 12 M. and 4 P. M.
For Wilmington, 7.30 A. M., 12 M. and 4 P. M.

FALL.

For Philadelphia, 7.30 A. M. and 3 P. M.
For Wilmington, 8 A. M. and 3 P. M.

WINTER.

For Philadelphia, 8 A. M.
For Wilmington, 3.30 P. M.

SPRING.

For Philadelphia, 7.30 A. M. and 3 P. M.
For Wilmington, 8.30 A. M. and 4 P. M.

Fare to Philadelphia or Wilmington 18¾ cents; return trips, Tickets 25 cents.

Salem Boats leave Chester as follows:—

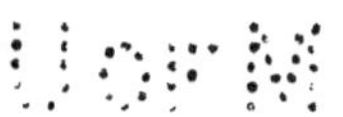

SUMMER.

For Salem, 10 A. M. and 3 P. M.
For Philadelphia, 9.30 A. M. and 4.30 P. M.

FALL, WINTER AND SPRING.

For Salem, 11 A. M.
For Philadelphia, 10.30 A. M.
Fare to Salem 50 cents, to Pennsgrove 25 cents, New Castle 50 cts., Delaware City 50 cts.

PHILADELPHIA WILMINGTON & BALTIMORE RAIL ROAD.

President—SAMUEL M. FELTON.

Directors—Moncure Robinson, Wm. L. Savage, Joseph C. Gilpin, John A. Duncan, Jesse Lane, *Wm. W.* Corcoran, Fred. A. Curtis, John C. Groome, J. S. Cohen, Jr., Thomas Kelso, Columbus O'Donnell, Enoch Pratt, Thomas Donaldson, Edward Austin.

Secretary & Treasurer—Alfred Horner.

Agent at Chester—Joseph Taylor.

Departure of Trains from Chester.

SOUTH:

Mail Train,--------------------8.45 A. M.
Express " ------------------12.28 P. M.
Accommodation Train,.-----------4.33 P. M.
Through Freight " -----------6.31 P. M.
Night Mail Train,--------------11.41 P. M.

NORTH:

Accommodation Train,-----------7.44 A. M.
Express Train,.----------------12.08 P. M.
Mail " ----------------2.27 P. M.
Night Mail Train,---------------9.18 P. M.

BUILDING ASSOCIATIONS.

CHESTER BUILDING ASSOCIATION.—Commenced Jan.

1850. Value of shares, $182 00. Paid in on each share, $117 00.

President—Fred. J. Hinkson.
Secretary—Joseph Taylor.
Treasurer—John K. Baker.

PENN BUILDING ASSOCIATION.—Commenced April 1853. Value of shares, $110 00. Paid in on each share, $80 00.

President—Perciphor Baker.
Secretary—William Hinkson.
Treasurer—Joseph H. Hinkson.

WASHINGTON BUILDING ASSOCIATION.—Commenced April, 1854. Value of shares, $93 00. Paid in on each share, $67 00.

President—Samuel H. Stevenson.
Secretary—Joseph Taylor.
Treasurer—Joseph H. Hinkson.

MASONS.

CHESTER LODGE, No. 236, OF ANCIENT YORK MASONS.—Instituted Dec. 4th, 1848. Meet on the Thursday evening on or before the full moon in each month, in Baker's Hall, Market and James streets. No. of members, 97. Officers

Worthy Master—Samuel Cliff.
Senior Warden—James Holmes, Jr.
Junior Warden—Daniel B. Thomson.
Treasurer—Edward H. Engle.
Secretary—William Hinkson.

ODD FELLOWS.

CHESTER LODGE, No. 92.—Meets in Penn Buildings, Market street, above James, every Wednesday evening. Date of Charter, Dec. 8th, 1843. No. of members, 45. Officers:

Noble Grand—Jno. A Temple.
Vice Grand—T. R. Long.
Secretary—James Riddle.
Assistant Secretary—E. R. Minshall.
Treasurer--Wm. H. Flavill.

UPLAND LODGE, No. 253.—Instituted June 21st, 1847. No. of members, 48. Installations the first meetings of April and October of every year. Meets every Saturday evening, in Penn Buildings, corner of Market Square. Officers:

Noble Grand—James Gartside.
Vice Grand—John Williams.
Secretary—William Kelley.
Assistant Secretary—William Hainsworth.
Treasurer—James Wilkie.

LEIPERVILLE LODGE, No. 263.—The hall in which it meets was built by a joint stock company of its members, and dedicated in 1853; it is situated at the corner of Broad and Mechanic streets. The Lodge was instituted Aug. 16th, 1847. Meets every Saturday evening. Installations the first Saturdays in April and May, of each year. No. of members, 114. Officers:

Noble Grand—John D. Scott.
Vice Grand—William Brewster.
Secretary—Nathan Y. Vanhorn.

CHESTER ENCAMPMENT, No. 99.—Instituted April 17th, 1850. No. of members, 25. Installations twice a year. Meets every second and fourth Tuesday evening of every month, in Penn Buildings, corner of Market Square. Officers:

Chief Patriarch.—Hugh Hutton.
High Priest.—Wm. H. Flavill.
Senior Warden—Charles Shroeder.
Junior Warden—Wm. L. Grubb.
Scribe—James Riddle.
Treasurer—James Wilkie.

RED MEN.

TUSCARORA TRIBE, No. 29, OF IMPROVED ORDER OF RED MEN.—Instituted in 1854. No. of members, 90. Installations first Mondays of January, April, July and October. Meetings every Monday evening, at seven o'clock in winter, and eight o'clock in summer.

Sachem—Joseph Taylor.
Senior Sagamore—Frank Cutler.
Junior Sagamore—Francis Besha.
Prophet—Humphrey Sneath.

JUNIOR SONS OF AMERICA.

Washington Camp No. 20. Instituted Dec. 19, 1854. Number of members 40. Installations the last week of March, June, September and December. Meets every Wednesday evening at Penn Buildings, corner of Market Square. Officers

Past President—Wm. R. Thatcher,
President—J. Henry Reifsnyder.
Secretary—Wm. H. H. Taylor.
Treasurer—Wm. H. Trout.
Master of Forms—Charles A. Story.
Ex. Past President—Edward C. Taylor.
Board of Correspondence—Wm. R. Thatcher, J. H. Reifsnyder, G. S. Riddle.

GAS WORKS.

Situated on the east side of Welsh street below James. Was built and put into operation in 1856. In 1858–9 about 1,483,000 cubic feet of gas was manufactured, and supplied to 220 consumers. The officers for the same year were

President—Frederick Fairlamb.
Managers--Fredk. Fairlamb, John O. Deshong, Samuel A. Crozier, John H. Baker, Robt. R. Dutton.
Secretary & Treasurer—John H. Baker.

WHARVES.

Pennsylvania Oil Company's wharf, west of Parker street. Gartside's wharf, between Fulton & Parker streets. Sinex's wharf, east of Fulton street. Irving's wharf, east of Franklin street. Booth's wharf, west of Essex. Smith's wharf, east of Essex. United States Front street wharf, foot of Edgmont street. United States Market street wharf and Steamboat Landing, foot of Market street.

DELAWARE COUNTY.

Length 16 m, breadth 11 m. Area 177 square m. Population in 1790, 9,483; in 1800, 12,809; in 1810, 14,734; in 1820, 14,810; in 1830, 17,323; 1840, 19,791; in 1850, 24,679.

CENSUS OF CHESTER FOR 1859.—Taken expressly for this work.

Whites—Males,	1865
" Females,	1927
Colored—Males,	142
" Females,	173
Total,	4107

ADVERTISEMENTS.

HINKSON & BAKER,

Lumber & Coal Merchants,

EDGMONT STREET,

(ADJOINING THE P. W. & B. RAILROAD.)

Have always on hand a superior article of

OF ALL THE DIFFERENT SIZES,

Prepared for Family and Steam purposes, which they will sell as low as the same article can be purchased elsewhere. They have also a general assortment of

DRY LUMBER

Of all kinds for Building,

To which they invite the attention of

CARPENTERS AND BUILDERS

IN WANT OF A FIRST-RATE ARTICLE, BEFORE PURCHASING ELSEWHERE.

WILLIAM HINKSON,
JOHN H. BAKER.

EDWARD R. MINSHALL,

GROCER & PROVISION DEALER,

COR. OF MARKET & WORK STREETS,

CHESTER, PA.

VEGETABLES OF ALL KINDS,

FOREIGN AND DOMESTIC FRUITS,

AND A VARIETY OF

Notions, Cedar-Ware, Churns, Buckets, Measures;

MUSICAL INSTRUMENTS, STRINGS, &c.

THOMAS W. BOWKER,

Plumber, Gas and Steam Fitter,

MANUFACTURER OF

Tin Copper & Sheet Iron Work;

CARD CANS

AND

CYLINDERS

FOR FACTORIES.

METALLIC ROOFING,

GUTTERING AND SPOUTING.

COR. OF MARKET & JAMES STS., CHESTER.

Drugs, Medicines, Paints, Oils,
DYE STUFFS, GLASS, HAIR OILS, POMADES,
COLOGNES, EXTRACTS, SOAPS, BRUSHES, &c.

LARKIN'S
ESSENCE OF JAMAICA GINGER,
Greatly Improved in Purity and Concentration, and will be found, on trial, an excellent Family Medicine, in Cramps, Colic, Flatulence or Stomach Derangement.

BOOKS, STATIONERY,
AND
WALL PAPER.

The subscriber has a good assortment of School & Miscellaneous Books and Stationery,

Deeds, Mortgages and Bonds,

Parchment Skin & Justice's Blanks,

Of the best quality. You will also find all the DAILY & WEEKLY PAPERS, and if you desire them sent to you, leave your order at the Book and Stationery Store of

J. WADE PRICE,

James Street, below Market, Chester, Pa.

☞ The Adams' Express arrives at Chester, **9.50** in the orning; **1.45** in the afternoon. ☜

www.ingramcontent.com/pod-product-compliance
Lightning Source LLC
LaVergne TN
LVHW021419110826
845150LV00007B/1989

9781425508845